D0945911

Writing

ISBN-13: 978-1-4190-3904-1
ISBN-10: 1-4190-3904-0

Steck-Vaughn is a trademark of Houghton Mifflin Harcourt
Supplemental Publishers

The paper used in this book comes from sustainable resources.

Printed in the United States of America.
2 3 4 5 6 7 8 9   862   14 13 12 11 10 09 08

www.SteckVaughn.com
800-531-5015

Core Skills Writing
Grade 6

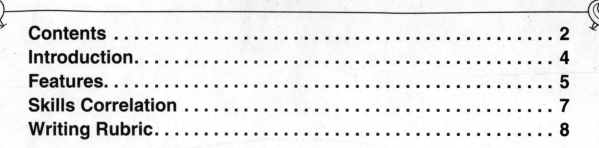

Unit 1: Laying the Foundation

Unit 2: Building Sentences

Unit 3: Building Paragraphs

Unit 4: Writing Forms

Blackline Masters

Introduction

Writing is one of the core skills necessary for success in school and in life. The better writer a person is, the better that person can communicate with others. Good writing is a skill acquired through guidance, practice, and self-evaluation. This book provides guidance for success in different writing formats. This book also provides many opportunities for writing practice. Finally, this book encourages writers to examine their own work and judge its qualities and flaws.

Clear writing and clear speaking are products of clear thinking. Clear thinking is a product of good organization of ideas. Good organization is a product of careful planning. One good way to plan is through graphic organizers.

- In this book, different kinds of graphic organizers are provided for students to plan their writing.
- One kind of graphic organizer, emphasized in Unit 2, allows writers to "see" their writing clearly.
- By "seeing" their writing, students can more easily determine how the different parts of a sentence work together to produce a clear expression of their main idea.
- This kind of graphic organizer allows students a more visual and tactile appreciation of their writing. It also appeals to multiple intelligences.

Language Arts Standards

The National Council of Teachers of English (NCTE) believes that "all students must have the opportunities and resources to develop the language skills they need to pursue life's goals and to participate fully as informed, productive members of society." The NCTE also feels that students must "apply a wide range of strategies as they write and use different writing process elements appropriately to communicate with different audiences for a variety of purposes."

The Skills Correlation Chart on page 7 allows for easy location of these skills and strategies in the book.

Organization

This book is divided into four units. Each unit builds upon earlier units. Using this scaffolded approach, writing becomes like construction. This book can help to build better writers.

- **Unit 1: Laying the Foundation** addresses basic concepts of writing, such as good writing traits and the process of writing.
- **Unit 2: Building Sentences** emphasizes the act of writing. Writers first deal with the main idea of a sentence, and then expand sentences by adding other parts of speech. By using graphic organizers, writers can visualize their sentences clearly.
- **Unit 3: Building Paragraphs** focuses on the structure and content of a well-written paragraph. Writers also learn about revising, proofreading, and self-evaluation in this unit.
- **Unit 4: Writing Forms** provides guidance and practice writing in different formats such as narration, description, persuasion, and informative reports.

Write Away

For too many students, writing is a struggle or a pain. They may not realize the benefits of being a good writer, or they may not care. This book tries to reach out to all writers with a light tone and an approach that allows students to "see" their writing in a new light. Writing does not have to be a chore. It can be fun. Students just have to be reminded that good writing can be their golden ticket to success in school and life.

4

Features

The title clearly identifies the skill.

Bullets highlight important points of the skill.

Examples model the skill.

Students creatively apply the skill in **WRITE AWAY.**

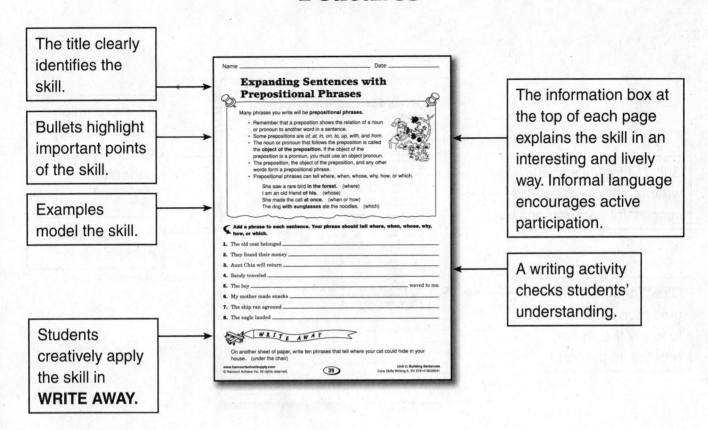

Expanding Sentences with Prepositional Phrases

Many phrases you write will be **prepositional phrases.**

- Remember that a preposition shows the relation of a noun or pronoun to another word in a sentence.
- Some prepositions are *of, at, in, on, to, up, with,* and *from.*
- The noun or pronoun that follows the preposition is called the **object of the preposition.** If the object of the preposition is a pronoun, you must use an object pronoun.
- The preposition, the object of the preposition, and any other words form a prepositional phrase.
- Prepositional phrases can tell where, when, whose, why, how, or which.

She saw a rare bird **in the forest.**   (where)
I am an old friend **of his.**   (whose)
She made the call **at once.**   (when or how)
The dog **with sunglasses** ate the noodles.   (which)

Add a phrase to each sentence. Your phrase should tell where, when, whose, why, how, or which.

1. The old coat belonged _____
2. They found their money _____
3. Aunt Chia will return _____
4. Sandy traveled _____
5. The boy _____ waved to me.
6. My mother made snacks _____
7. The ship ran aground _____
8. The eagle landed _____

WRITE AWAY

On another sheet of paper, write ten phrases that tell where your cat could hide in your house.   (under the chair)

www.harcourtschoolsupply.com
© Harcourt Achieve Inc. All rights reserved.

39

Unit 2: Building Sentences
Core Skills Writing 6, SV 9781419039041

The information box at the top of each page explains the skill in an interesting and lively way. Informal language encourages active participation.

A writing activity checks students' understanding.

Checklists guide students through the writing process.

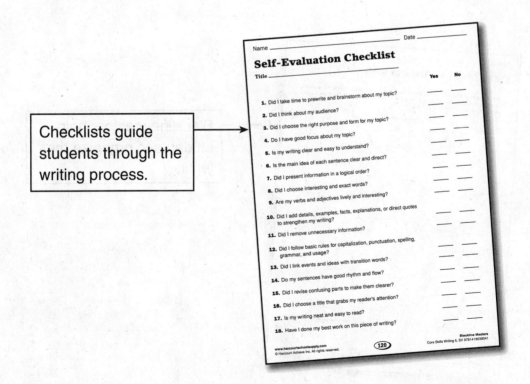

Self-Evaluation Checklist

Title _____

                                                          Yes   No

1. Did I take time to prewrite and brainstorm about my topic?
2. Did I think about my audience?
3. Did I choose the right purpose and form for my topic?
4. Do I have good focus about my topic?
5. Is my writing clear and easy to understand?
6. Is the main idea of each sentence clear and direct?
7. Did I present information in a logical order?
8. Did I choose interesting and exact words?
9. Are my verbs and adjectives lively and interesting?
10. Did I add details, examples, facts, explanations, or direct quotes to strengthen my writing?
11. Did I remove unnecessary information?
12. Did I follow basic rules for capitalization, punctuation, spelling, grammar, and usage?
13. Did I link events and ideas with transition words?
14. Do my sentences have good rhythm and flow?
15. Did I revise confusing parts to make them clearer?
16. Did I choose a title that grabs my reader's attention?
17. Is my writing neat and easy to read?
18. Have I done my best work on this piece of writing?

www.harcourtschoolsupply.com
© Harcourt Achieve Inc. All rights reserved.

120

Blackline Masters
Core Skills Writing 6, SV 9781419039041

Features

Bullets identify specific writing hints to assure successful paragraphs.

Directions provide guidance on how to apply the writing process to the form.

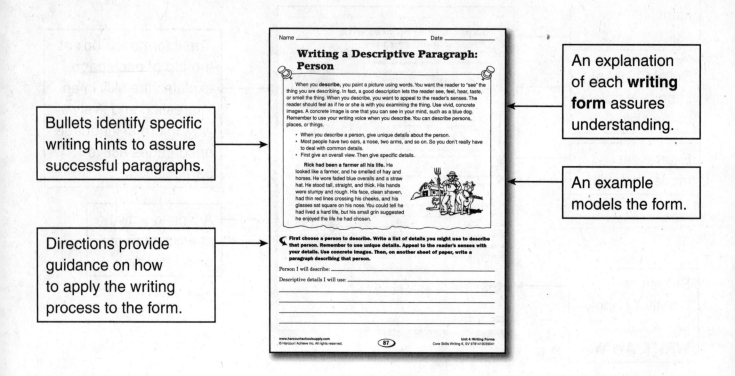

An explanation of each **writing form** assures understanding.

An example models the form.

Writing a Descriptive Paragraph: Person

When you **describe**, you paint a picture using words. You want the reader to "see" the thing you are describing. In fact, a good description lets the reader see, feel, hear, taste, or smell the thing. When you describe, you want to appeal to the reader's senses. The reader should feel as if he or she is with you examining the thing. Use vivid, concrete images. A concrete image is one that you can see in your mind, such as a blue dog. Remember to use your writing voice when you describe. You can describe persons, places, or things.

- When you describe a person, give unique details about the person.
- Most people have two ears, a nose, two arms, and so on. So you don't really have to deal with common details.
- First give an overall view. Then give specific details.

Rick had been a farmer all his life. He looked like a farmer, and he smelled of hay and horses. He wore faded blue overalls and a straw hat. He stood tall, straight, and thick. His hands were stumpy and rough. His face, clean shaven, had thin red lines crossing his cheeks, and his glasses sat square on his nose. You could tell he had lived a hard life, but his small grin suggested he enjoyed the life he had chosen.

First choose a person to describe. Write a list of details you might use to describe that person. Remember to use unique details. Appeal to the reader's senses with your details. Use concrete images. Then, on another sheet of paper, write a paragraph describing that person.

Person I will describe: _____

Descriptive details I will use: _____

_____

_____

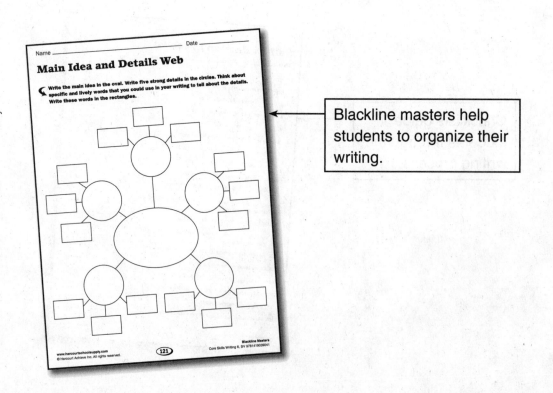

Main Idea and Details Web

Write the main idea in the oval. Write five strong details in the circles. Think about specific and lively words that you could use in your writing to tell about the details. Write these words in the rectangles.

Blackline masters help students to organize their writing.

Skills Correlation

Skill	Page
Vocabulary	
Word Choice	20, 32, 33, 34, 54, 57, 58
Figurative Language	60, 61
Sentences	
Word Order in Sentences	62
Recognizing Sentences and Sentence Types	47, 48, 49, 50
Main Idea of Sentence	25, 31
Subjects and Predicates	25, 26, 27, 28, 29, 31, 42, 43, 46, 53
Compound/Complex Sentences	50
Sentence Combining	52, 53, 54
Sentence Fragments	64
Run-on Sentences	65, 66
Clauses and Phrases	37, 38, 39, 40, 44, 45
Independent and Dependent Clauses	37, 38, 45
Compound Subjects and Predicates	42, 43, 53
Objects	27, 31
Predicate Nominatives and Predicate Adjectives	29, 30
Sentence Variety	57, 58, 59, 62, 63
Grammar and Usage	
Common and Proper Nouns	13
Singular and Plural Nouns	13
Possessive Nouns	13
Verbs and Verb Tense	14, 56
Subject-Verb Agreement	26, 43
Verb Phrases	28
Active and Passive Voice Verbs	14, 55
Pronouns	13
Adjectives	15, 30, 32, 33, 34, 57, 58, 59
Adverbs	15, 35
Prepositions	16, 38, 39, 40, 46
Prepositional Phrases	38, 39, 40, 46
Conjunctions	16, 41, 42, 43, 44, 45, 46, 51, 52, 53
Capitalization and Punctuation	
Capitalization: First Word in Sentence	24
Capitalization: Proper Nouns	13
End Punctuation	47, 48, 49
Commas	51, 52, 54
Quotation Marks	92, 109

Skill	Page
Composition	
Expanding Sentences	32, 33, 34, 35, 36, 37, 38, 39, 40, 41, 52, 53, 54
Paragraphs: Topic Sentence (main idea)	69, 70, 71, 74, 76, 124
Paragraphs: Supporting Details	69, 70, 72, 76, 124
Paragraph: Concluding Sentence	69, 70, 73, 124
Order in Paragraphs	69, 78
Writing Process	
Audience	10, 18, 20, 21, 114, 115
Purpose	11, 114, 115
Voice	20, 75, 116
Prewriting and Brainstorming	17, 74, 114, 115
Topic	17, 19, 22, 70, 71, 82
Organization and Form	11, 19, 76, 77, 78, 79, 80, 81, 87, 88, 89, 90, 91, 92, 93, 94, 95, 96, 97, 98, 99, 100, 101, 102, 103, 104, 105, 106, 107, 108, 109, 110, 111, 112, 113, 114, 121, 122, 123, 124
Outlining	110, 111
Note Taking	108, 109
Drafting	17, 23
Revising and Proofreading	18, 21, 23, 64, 65, 66, 68, 83, 84, 86, 118, 119, 120
Publishing	18, 21, 85, 117
Types of Writing	
Descriptive Paragraph	87, 88, 89
Narrative Paragraph	90, 91, 92
Persuasive Paragraph	99, 100, 101
Information Paragraph	96, 97, 98
Definition Paragraph	95
Comparing and Contrasting	79, 93, 94
Cause and Effect	80, 123
Problem and Solution	81, 123
Summary	77, 108, 122
Literary Response	102, 103
Informative Report	107, 108, 109, 110, 111, 112, 113
Writing for Tests	104, 105, 106

Writing Rubric

Score of 4

The student:

- clearly and completely addresses the writing task,
- demonstrates an understanding of the purpose for writing,
- maintains a single focus,
- presents a main idea supported by relevant details,
- uses paragraphs to organize main ideas and supporting ideas under the umbrella of a thesis statement,
- presents content in a logical order and sequence,
- uses variety in sentence types, beginnings, and lengths,
- chooses the correct writing pattern and form to communicate ideas clearly,
- clearly portrays feelings through voice and word choice,
- uses language appropriate to the writing task, such as language rich in sensory details in a descriptive passage,
- uses vocabulary to suit purpose and audience,
- summarizes main ideas in a concluding paragraph when appropriate, such as in an information report,
- establishes and defends a position in a persuasive paragraph, and
- has few or no errors in the standard rules of English grammar, punctuation, capitalization, and spelling.

Score of 3

The student:

- generally follows the criteria described above, and
- has some errors in the standard rules of English grammar, punctuation, capitalization, and spelling, but not enough to impair the reader's comprehension.

Score of 2

The student:

- marginally follows the criteria described above, and
- has several errors in the standard rules of English grammar, punctuation, capitalization, and spelling that may impair a reader's comprehension.

Score of 1

The student:

- fails to follow the criteria described above, and
- has many errors in the standard rules of English grammar, punctuation, capitalization, and spelling that impair a reader's comprehension.

Name _____ Date _____

Why Write?

Do you like to write? Many people say they don't. They think they can speak everything they need to communicate. Can they? Maybe, but sometimes writing is better than talking. How is writing better than talking?

- When you write, you have more time to think about your ideas.
- You can organize your ideas better when you write them down.
- You can make your ideas more permanent by writing them on paper.
- Writing takes your place when you are not there to talk.

In fact, writing is really much like talking. When you write or talk, you use ideas. You use the different parts of speech. You often use complete sentences. And your goal is the same for both methods—to communicate with others. Writing can be fun, too. Just think, in twenty or thirty years you can read something you wrote in the sixth grade. Won't that be interesting?

Darken the circle by the answer that best completes each sentence.

1. You can make your ideas _____ by writing them on paper.

Ⓐ better Ⓑ more intelligent
Ⓒ funnier Ⓓ more permanent

2. When you write, you have time to _____ your ideas better.

Ⓐ confuse Ⓑ organize
Ⓒ forget Ⓓ erase

3. You have time to _____ before you write your ideas on paper.

Ⓐ see a movie Ⓑ think more
Ⓒ sleep Ⓓ find your pen

4. Writing can take your _____ when you aren't available to speak.

Ⓐ place Ⓑ lunch
Ⓒ seat Ⓓ money

WRITE AWAY

Do you like writing or talking better? Think about the question for a while. Discuss your ideas with a friend or family member. Then, in your best writing, tell which you like better and why. Use another sheet of paper.

Unit 1: Laying the Foundation
Core Skills Writing 6, SV 9781419039041

What to Write

Wouldn't it be great if words could just magically appear on paper? Since this doesn't happen, you have to think about what you write. You might have an assignment to write or need to give someone directions. You might also want to write a list, a poem, or a letter to a friend. There are many things you can write. Before you do, though, you must decide three things.

1. **Who is your audience?** Your audience is your reader. Are you writing for yourself? Your friends or family? A teacher? Your community? Before you write, ask yourself questions to target your audience.

   - Who will read what I write?
   - What do I know about these people?
   - What do I have to say to the readers?
   - Why do I want the readers to care about my writing?
   - Am I writing about opinions or about facts?
   - Will my writing be funny or serious, happy or sad?

Name a possible audience for each piece of writing.

1. a sad poem about a lost pet

_____

2. a report about traffic problems

_____

3. an invitation to a dinner party

_____

4. a book review

_____

5. a funny story about an uncle

_____

6. an election speech

_____

WRITE AWAY

Would a letter you write to your grandparents be different from a letter you write to a friend? How would the letters be different? Write a few sentences about your ideas.

_____

_____

_____

What to Write, page 2

2. **Why are you writing?** Before you write, you must choose a **purpose,** or goal, for your writing. Writers have four main purposes:

    • to **express** personal feelings or ideas   (opinions, diary, journal)
    • to **inform**   (facts, report, research paper)
    • to **entertain** others   (story, poem, joke)
    • to **persuade** others   (speech, book review)

3. **How will you organize your writing?** Your audience and your purpose determine how you will organize your writing. To be an effective writer, you must choose the correct form to achieve your purpose. This book presents many forms you can use to write.

What purpose would you use to write each of the following? Darken the circle by your choice.

1. a humorous story about sharks

   Ⓐ express   Ⓑ entertain

   Ⓒ persuade   Ⓓ inform

2. your feelings about a favorite friend

   Ⓐ express   Ⓑ entertain

   Ⓒ persuade   Ⓓ inform

3. a speech for a national election

   Ⓐ express   Ⓑ entertain

   Ⓒ persuade   Ⓓ inform

4. a report about Egypt

   Ⓐ express   Ⓑ entertain

   Ⓒ persuade   Ⓓ inform

WRITE AWAY

You want to watch TV before you do your homework. How can you get this to happen?

What purpose would you use? _____

Who would your audience be? _____

         Core Skills Writing 6, SV 9781419039041

Keeping a Journal

Jour is a French word that means "day." A **journal** is a record of daily events. In a journal, you can write about your ideas, thoughts, and feelings. You can write stories or poems in your journal. You can draw pictures. You can do anything you want in your journal. It's your special place. And journals can be fun to read when you get older. You can make your journal better by doing these things.

- Write the date.
- Write about important events that happened today.
- Tell why the events are important to you.
- Write poems or stories about the events. Illustrate them.

Here's a sample:

December 14, 2007   Last night I went out around midnight and looked at the sky. Overhead, the Geminids meteor shower was taking place. I saw dozens of meteors, or shooting stars. It was cool. In fact, it was freezing out there. Ha, ha!

Write a short journal entry about something important that happened to you today. Use another sheet of paper if necessary.

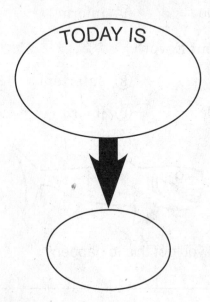

TODAY IS

_____
_____
_____
_____
_____
_____
_____
_____

WRITE AWAY

Start your own journal. Use a notebook. Write the date. Write your feelings and ideas. Write poems and stories about your daily life. Writing your personal feelings can help you understand them better.

Primary Parts of Speech

Two of the most important parts of speech are **nouns** and **pronouns.** Nouns and pronouns are used for naming. A noun is a word that names a person, place, or thing.

- A **common noun** names any person, place, or thing (man, bridge, bus). A common noun begins with a small letter.
- A **proper noun** names a specific person, place, or thing (Karey, London, Yellowstone Park). A proper noun begins with a capital letter.
- Nouns can be singular, plural, or possessive (dog, dogs, dog's).

Pronouns take the place of nouns. Be sure the noun the pronoun refers to is clear to the reader. Use pronouns to avoid repeating words.

- A **subject pronoun** is used as the subject of a sentence (I, we, they, he, she, who).
- An **object pronoun** is used as the object of a sentence (me, us, them, him, her, whom).
- Pronouns can be singular, plural, or possessive (it, they, my).

Write nouns or pronouns to fit each writing need.

1. What nouns could you use to write about your home?

_____

2. What nouns could you use to write about a grocery store?

_____

3. What nouns could you use to write about sports?

_____

4. What pronouns could you use to write about yourself?

_____

5. What pronouns could you use to write about your friends or family?

_____

On another sheet of paper, write a list of 20 common nouns. Beside each common noun, write a proper noun that names the thing described by the common noun.

Name _____ Date _____

Primary Parts of Speech, page 2

A **verb** is another important part of speech. A verb shows action or connects the subject to another word in a sentence. Verbs can be **action verbs, linking verbs,** or **helping verbs.** Verbs can be singular or plural. They can be active or passive.

Verbs are also used to tell the time something is happening. The time a verb shows is called tense.

- A present tense verb tells what is happening now.   (call)
- A past tense verb tells what happened in the past.   (called)
- A future tense verb tells what will happen in the future.   (will call)

Write verbs to fit each writing need.

1. What verbs could you use to write about running a race?

_____

2. What verbs could you use to write about what you do at home?

_____

3. What verbs could you use to write about chores you must do?

_____

4. What verbs could you use to write about a vacation last year?

_____

5. What verbs could you use to write about a vacation next year?

_____

W R I T E   A W A Y

What are some verbs that tell how you can use your fingers? (snap, hold)
On another sheet of paper, write a list of all the verbs you can think of.

Modifiers

Adjectives and **adverbs** are two more parts of speech. Adjectives and adverbs are **modifiers.** A modifier is a word or group of words that modifies, or changes, the meaning of another word.

cat ——————▶ **black** cat

- An adjective modifies a noun or pronoun.

    gray clouds   **funny** movie   **grateful** me

- An adverb modifies a verb, an adjective, or another adverb.

    talked **quickly**   **quite** talented   **very** cautiously

Write adjectives or adverbs to fit each writing need.

1. What adjectives could you use to write about autumn?

_____

2. What adjectives could you use to write about your neighborhood?

_____

3. What adjectives could you use to write about water?

_____

4. What adverbs could you use to write about the way you sing?

_____

5. What adverbs could you use to write about the way babies move?

_____

6. What adverbs could you use to write about the way people talk?

_____

W R I T E   A W A Y

On another sheet of paper, draw a picture. You can use a pencil, a pen, or crayons. Then write at least twelve adjectives that describe your picture.

Name _____ Date _____

Connectives

Conjunctions and **prepositions** are two more parts of speech. Conjunctions and prepositions are **connectives**. Connectives join parts of a sentence.

- A conjunction connects words or groups of words. A coordinate conjunction joins words of equal rank. Some coordinate conjunctions are *and, or, but,* and *yet.* A subordinate conjunction joins groups of words of unequal rank. Some subordinate conjunctions are *because, before, that,* and *which.*

    night **and** day   left **or** right
    I left **before** the store closed.

- A preposition shows the relation of a noun or pronoun to another word in a sentence. Some common prepositions are *of, at, in, on, to, up, near, from, by,* and *into.*

    The book is **on** my desk.

Write a coordinate or subordinate conjunction to complete each sentence.

1. I felt sick _____ I rode the roller coaster.

2. The night air was cold, _____ the rain kept falling.

3. The hikers lost their way, _____ they kept on moving.

4. Omar did not go to the movie _____ he had no money.

5. I did my homework _____ I went to the game.

6. Kara could go to Europe next summer, _____ she could get a job.

Write two prepositions that have a meaning similar to the given word.

7. beneath _____

8. near _____

W R I T E   A W A Y

Think of prepositions that tell a location, such as *above* or *beside.* Write as many as you can on another sheet of paper.

The Writing Process

Have you ever sat and stared at a blank sheet of paper? You just couldn't think of anything to write or didn't know where to begin. This is not unusual. Many people have the same problem. The following steps, however, can help you fill that blank paper with wonderful words.

1. Prewriting

Prewriting is sometimes called **brainstorming.** It is the step in which you think about what and why you are writing. You choose a purpose and an audience. You choose a **topic** and make a list of your ideas. Then you organize your ideas so they make sense. Many writers use outlines or graphic organizers. The Prewriting Survey on pages 114 and 115 can help you plan your writing.

Suppose you must eat a worm sandwich for lunch. You decide to write about it in your journal. Use the organizer to help you prewrite.

Nouns I might use: _____

Verbs I might use: _____

Adjectives I might use: _____

Adverbs I might use: _____

2. Drafting

In the drafting step, writers put their ideas on paper. They write words, ideas, and sentences. Some parts of the draft may have too much information. Other parts may not have enough information. There are often many mistakes in this step of the writing process. But that's OK! A draft should not be perfect. You just want to get all of your ideas on paper. You concentrate on what you want to say, and you correct your mistakes later.

Write a sentence you might include in your journal about eating a worm sandwich. Use some of the words you wrote above. Think about your sentence for a while, and then write the sentence again using different words or a different order.

_____

_____

_____

The Writing Process, page 2

3. Revising

Revising means "seeing again." In the revising step, you "see" your draft again. You read your work carefully to be sure it makes sense. You may uncover new ways to express yourself. You may find new ways to arrange your ideas. You can add or remove details to make the writing clearer. You can often hear problems when you read your writing aloud. Ask someone else to read your work and give you suggestions for improvement.

4. Proofreading

When you proofread, you read your writing carefully to find mistakes. You should read your work once for capital letters and punctuation. You should read it a second time for spelling. You should read it a third time for verb tense and subject-verb agreement. You should read it a fourth time for sentence structure. Use the Proofreading Checklist on page 118 as a guide. A list of Proofreading Marks can be found on page 119.

Proofread the following sentence. Make corrections. Then write the corrected sentence on the line.

A fury bare fished in the mountun streem.

_____

5. Publishing

Publishing your writing is fun. Publishing means "to make public." You can present your writing to your teacher, to your friends, to your family, or to the community. You can read it orally, post it on a Web site, or make it into a book. First, make a clean copy of your writing. You can handwrite it or type it on the computer. Then, add pictures, a cover, and a title page if you like. Now the writing is ready to share!

Read the steps in the writing process. Write numbers 1 through 5 to show the correct order.

_____ Make a clean copy of your writing to share with others.

_____ Write your first draft to get your ideas on paper.

_____ Proofread your writing to check for spelling and grammar errors.

_____ Read your writing carefully to be sure it makes sense.

_____ Choose a topic to write about and make notes.

Name _____ Date _____

The Seven Traits of Good Writing

When you write, you have a **purpose,** or reason, for writing. You might want to express your feelings or opinions. You might want to inform or entertain your reader. You might try to convince your reader. There are seven **writing traits,** or skills, that can help you achieve your purpose. These writing traits can help you become a better writer.

1. Ideas

You write about your **ideas,** or thoughts on a topic. What you have to say is important, and you most likely want to share your ideas with others. When you write, you must be sure that the readers understand your message. You want them to be interested in your message, too. So, you must be sure your ideas make sense. Include enough details to make your ideas clear to the reader. Good ideas show good thinking.

2. Organization

The **organization** of your writing is the way you group your ideas and details. First, you must choose the correct form of writing for your purpose. E-mail messages, letters, stories, reports, and journals are some writing forms. Next, your writing should have good structure. Are your ideas written in a logical order? Do you have a beginning, middle, and end? Do your paragraphs have strong topic sentences? Finally, check your very first sentence. Does it grab the reader's attention? If so, the reader will keep reading. That's important! Where would a writer be without a reader?

Answer each question.

1. You want to tell a relative about how you are doing in school. What are some ideas you could include?

_____

_____

2. What form of organization would you choose to tell your relative about your school performance? Would you write a report? A story? A letter? Identify the form you would use.

_____

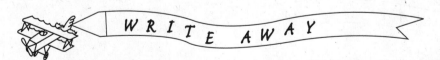

WRITE AWAY

How is a story like a poem? How are they different? Brainstorm your ideas with a friend or family member. Then write two or three sentences about your ideas on another sheet of paper.

The Seven Traits of Good Writing, page 2

3. Voice

When you are happy, you smile and laugh. When you are angry, you might shout loudly. When you talk, people can tell by your voice how you feel. They know if you are happy, sad, or angry. As a writer, you want to let the reader know what you are feeling, too. You can show these feelings through the words you choose and the sentences you write. You use a writing **voice.** To share a happy feeling, you write about ideas that are happy. You choose words that are happy. When you use the writing trait of voice, you make the reader feel the way you do. Your writing voice replaces your speaking voice.

What voice would you use if your best friend moved away?

_____

4. Word Choice

You know that you can choose words to make your readers feel a certain way. **Word choice** is important in other ways, too. You must be sure the reader clearly understands what you are writing about. You should choose exact words to explain an idea. Words that appeal to the senses help readers draw a mental picture of your writing. The reader should be able to see, hear, taste, smell, and touch your ideas by reading your words. You should also choose exact words and strong action verbs to explain an idea. Did you see a dog or did you see a fuzzy, white poodle? Did the squirrel go up the tree or scamper up the tree?

What words could you choose to show you are sad because your best friend moved away?

_____

_____

WRITE AWAY

What are some words that you could use to describe a squealing, smelly pig? Write your words on another sheet of paper.

The Seven Traits of Good Writing, page 3

5. Sentence Fluency

Sentence fluency is when the sentences in your text flow smoothly and have a rhythm. You can do this by changing the length of your sentences. You can also write sentences that have different patterns. Some sentences might begin with a noun. Others might begin with a preposition or an adjective. Read your sentences aloud. Do they flow or stumble?

Write a sentence that you think has good fluency.

_____

6. Conventions

The **conventions** are all the rules of grammar and writing. Does every sentence in your writing begin with a capital letter? Does each sentence have the correct end punctuation? Is each sentence complete? Are the words spelled correctly? Follow the rules to correct the mistakes in your writing.

7. Presentation

Presentation is the way your words and pictures look on the page. Your work should look neat. It should be easy to read. The pictures should show important ideas. And don't forget a good title! A good title makes readers want to read your writing.

Would you want to read a book named The Story? Why or why not?

_____

_____

You will use these writing traits all through the writing process. There is a lot of information here to remember. You may be feeling a bit anxious about writing. Don't worry, though. It's just writing. You do, however, want to do your best work. You can use the Writing Traits Checklist on pages 116 and 117 to help you become a better writer.

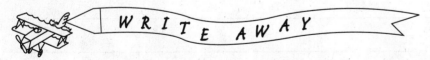

How can a title make you want to read a book or watch a movie? What is your favorite title of a book or movie? Why did that title make you want to read or watch? Brainstorm your ideas with a friend or family member. Write your ideas on another sheet of paper.

Name _____   Date _____

Basic Rules of Writing

When you write, you can let your imagination run wild. You can think deeply about different topics. You can write about your most personal feelings or create fantasy lands. As a writer, you can change the way you express yourself. You can use different words and experiment with new topics. If you don't like what you write, you can throw it away and start over. You never stop learning how to write. It is a fun and rewarding process. Here are a few basic rules to improve your writing.

Write What You Know

Write about things that interest you, if possible. What kinds of things do you know a lot about? Try writing about one of these topics. You will write better if you understand and feel strongly about your topic. Your reader will know that what you've written is important to you. Sometimes you will have to write about things that don't really interest you. A good writer can make even dull things seem interesting! Remember your writing voice.

What do you know a lot about? Make a list of topics you could write about.

_____

_____

_____

Stick to the Topic

Once you choose a topic, you must keep your writing focused on that topic. Decide what your readers need to know about your topic. If you're writing about an animal, focus on what it looks like. Give details about how it acts and what it eats. Don't let your writing wander off to some other topic. One way to stick to the topic is to organize. Make an outline of what you want to write. You can write an outline on paper or create one in your mind. You should have a good idea of what you want to write before you begin to write.

If you were writing about rivers in Europe, would it be a good idea to include information about the Missouri River? Why or why not?

_____

_____

_____

_____

_____

Core Skills Writing 6, SV 9781419039041

Basic Rules of Writing, page 2

Drafts

After you organize, you are ready to write the first draft. You should plan to write two or three drafts. When you write your first draft, you should write as though you are telling a story to your friends. Give all the details, but don't worry about how you sound. Don't worry about mistakes or neatness. The important thing is to put your ideas on paper. You can organize them better in later drafts. You can add or remove details later, too.

Write a sentence about your favorite possession. Write quickly. Pretend this sentence is your first draft.

_____

_____

Reread and Edit

You don't have to be a perfect speller to be a good writer. You don't need to know all the rules of grammar, either. But you should correct as many errors as you can. Read your work over and over until you have fixed your mistakes. Try reading your work aloud. That way, both your eyes and your ears can help you catch problems. Use the Proofreading Checklist on page 118 to help you find errors. When you have corrected as many problems as you can, you are ready to write your final draft.

Read aloud the sentence you wrote above. How does it sound? Can it be improved? Are there mistakes in your sentence? Edit your sentence. Write the second draft of your sentence below.

_____

_____

What are the strengths and weaknesses of your writing? What are some other ways you can improve your writing? Write your ideas below.

_____

_____

_____

_____

Name _____ Date _____

What Is a Sentence?

A **sentence** is a group of words that expresses a complete thought. It begins with a capital letter and ends with a punctuation mark. A sentence has two main parts, a **subject** and a **predicate**.

- The subject tells who or what the sentence is about.
- The **complete subject** is all the words in the subject.

    My friends came to my party.

- The predicate tells what the subject is or does.
- The **complete predicate** is all the words in the predicate.

    My friends **came to my party.**

 Are the words below sentences? Write *yes* or *no*.

_____ **1.** A computer in the library.

_____ **2.** Reeta reads poems in the park.

_____ **3.** Howling coyotes near the woods.

_____ **4.** Tara told Thomas a tall tale.

_____ **5.** Dropped down into a deep, dark cave.

Write a word or words on the line to make each sentence complete.

6. _____ found a fox in a trap.

7. _____ wrote a story about whales.

8. Carlos and Chad _____.

9. The old dog _____.

10. The new worker _____.

W R I T E   A W A Y

On another sheet of paper, write six short sentences like those above. Include a subject or a predicate and a line for the other part. Trade with a friend or family member. Complete each other's sentences.

Unit 2: Building Sentences
Core Skills Writing 6, SV 9781419039041

The Main Idea of a Sentence

The simple subject and simple predicate form the **main idea** of the sentence. The simple subject and the simple predicate can stand alone as a complete sentence.

- The **simple subject** is the main noun or pronoun in the complete subject.
- The **simple predicate** is the main verb in the complete predicate.

Ducks quack.	**Ducks**	**quack**
	subject	predicate

⟵ main idea line

You can use a graphic organizer to make a diagram of the sentence. Separate the subject from the predicate with a bar. Capitalize the first word of the sentence in the diagram.

➤ **Read the poem below. Complete the last two lines of the poem by writing a predicate on the line. Try to make rhymes. Then write two of the sentences in the graphic organizers.**

Bells ring.

Horses prance.

Singers _____.

Dancers _____.

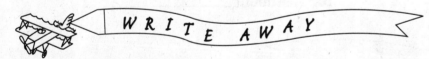

W R I T E   A W A Y

On another sheet of paper, write a poem about the sounds animals make. Then write each sentence in a graphic organizer that you draw.

Name _____ Date _____

Subject-Verb Agreement

The verb you use as the simple predicate in a sentence must agree in number with the simple subject.

- Use a **singular verb** when the simple subject is singular.

  An owl hoots.   a singular verb for a singular subject

- Use a **plural verb** when the simple subject is plural.

  Owls hoot.   a plural verb for a plural subject

Write a subject or verb as needed to complete each sentence. Be sure that the subject and verb agree in number.

1. Sharks _____.

2. Lightning _____.

3. Dogs _____.

4. A baby _____.

5. _____ smell.

6. _____ scratch.

7. _____ roll.

8. The _____ howls.

9. Leaves _____.

10. A student _____.

Put on your thinking cap. Some nouns can be both singular and plural. One example is *deer*. How many others do you know? Write a list below.

_____

_____

_____

_____

_____

Unit 2: Building Sentences
Core Skills Writing 6, SV 9781419039041

Name _____ Date _____

Direct Objects

The main idea of your sentence may include a **direct object.** A direct object follows an action verb. It receives the action of the verb. It is part of the complete predicate. The direct object will be a noun or a pronoun.

People fly airplanes.

People	fly	airplanes

With a graphic organizer, you can easily see the main idea of the sentence. A long bar separates the simple subject from the simple predicate. A shorter bar separates the simple predicate from the direct object.

Write a direct object to complete each sentence. Then write two of the sentences in the graphic organizers below. Be sure to write the subject, predicate, and object in the correct place.

1. Harrison hit _____.

2. Lions chase _____.

3. Students write _____.

4. Bears eat _____.

5. Karla called _____.

6. The fire burned _____.

7. My uncle lost _____.

8. We need _____.

On another sheet of paper, write five sentences that contain direct objects. Circle the object in each sentence. Then write each sentence in a graphic organizer that you draw.

Helping Verbs

Sometimes a main verb is lazy. It needs a helper to show action and time. A **helping verb** comes before the main verb in a sentence. The main verb and its helpers form a **verb phrase.** The last verb in a verb phrase is the main verb. Some common helping verbs are *am, is, are, was, were, will, must, can, may, have,* and *do.*

helping   main
verbs   verb

Maria **may have fainted.**

verb phrase

The subject and verb phrase form the main idea of the sentence. The main idea may include a direct object.

Ron **can repair radios.**

Ron	can repair	radios

Write a helping verb on the line to complete each sentence. Then write the first and last sentences on the graphic organizers below.

1. We _____ visiting New York.

2. I _____ enjoying the museums.

3. _____ you like big cities?

4. My brother _____ moving to Phoenix.

5. Faith _____ win the race.

_____|_____|_____   _____|_____|_____

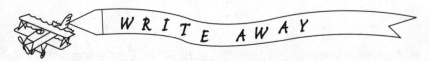

W R I T E   A W A Y

On another sheet of paper, write five sentences that contain helping verbs. Include direct objects in some of your sentences. Then draw five graphic organizers and write your sentences in the organizers. Be sure to write each part in the correct place.

Name _____   Date _____

Linking Verbs

You probably know what a **linking verb** does. If you said that it links, you're right. A linking verb links the subject to a noun or an adjective in the complete predicate. The noun renames the subject, or the adjective describes the subject. Some linking verbs are *is, are, was, were, am,* and *been.* Some linking verbs can also be action verbs. These include *feel, look, seem, smell,* and *taste.*

If the verb links the subject to a noun or pronoun, that noun or pronoun is called a **predicate nominative.** If the verb links the subject to an adjective, that adjective is called a **predicate adjective.**

They <u>**are friends.**</u>   ⟵   (predicate nominative)
Samuel <u>**seems** seasick.</u>   ⟵   (predicate adjective)

The predicate nominative and predicate adjective are part of the main idea of the sentence. When you write them in a graphic organizer, they go in the same place as the direct object. But the short bar leans back toward the subject. This leaning bar shows that the predicate nominative or predicate adjective is linked to the subject.

They | are \ friends   Samuel | seems \ seasick

Write a linking verb to complete each sentence. Then write the sentence on the graphic organizer.

1. The painting _____ beautiful.   _____|_____

2. The perfume _____ wonderful.   _____|_____

3. Eddie _____ unhappy.   _____|_____

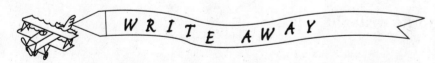

On another sheet of paper, write six short sentences that contain linking verbs. Include a predicate nominative or predicate adjective in each sentence. Then draw six graphic organizers and write your sentences in the organizers.

Name _____ Date _____

Predicate Nominatives and Predicate Adjectives

• You know that a linking verb links the subject to a noun or an adjective in the complete predicate. If the verb links the subject to a noun or pronoun, that noun or pronoun is called a predicate nominative. Predicate nominatives can be common or proper nouns.

My brothers are **carpenters.**   My favorite city is **San Antonio.**

When the predicate nominative is a pronoun, you must use a subject pronoun.

Who is the winner?   The winner is **I.**

If the verb links the subject to an adjective, that adjective is called a predicate adjective. Predicate adjectives can be common or proper adjectives.

Andy is **quiet.**   Andy is **British.**

Write a predicate nominative noun to complete each sentence.

1. Terrell is a talented _____.

2. That man was a _____.

3. She is the fastest _____ on the track.

4. Her mother is a famous _____.

Write a predicate nominative pronoun to complete each sentence. Be sure to use a subject pronoun.

5. The best singer was _____.

6. My favorite person is _____.

7. _____ is your favorite writer?

Write a predicate adjective to complete each sentence.

8. Everyone became _____ after the delay.

9. The food smells _____.

10. Their house is _____.

11. Many gases are _____.

Review: The Main Idea of a Sentence

The main idea of a sentence is the most important part of the sentence. It tells the most important information in the sentence.

- The main idea may include only a simple subject and a simple predicate.
  Sara sings.

- The main idea may include a simple subject, a simple predicate, and a direct object.   **Sara sings songs.**

- The main idea can include a subject, a linking verb, and a linked noun, pronoun, or adjective.   **Sara is a singer.   She seems satisfied.**

Remember where each part of the sentence belongs in the graphic organizer.

| subject | verb | object | | subject | verb | predicate nominative or adjective |

Write a sentence that will fit each graphic organizer below. Write your sentence on the organizer. Then write your sentence on the line.

1. _____

_____

2. _____

_____

3. _____

_____

4. _____

_____

5. _____

Adding Details to Sentences

The main idea tells the most important part of a sentence. But you may want to include more information in your sentence. You can add **details.** Details tell more about the main idea. Details can tell whose, which, when, where, and how. Details make your sentence more interesting.

A hungry duck ate **my ketchup** sandwich.

You can see the main idea of the sentence in the graphic organizer below. All the parts of the main idea go above the main idea line. All the details go below the line. *A, hungry, my,* and *ketchup* are adjectives that modify nouns in the sentence. Place the adjectives under the words they modify.

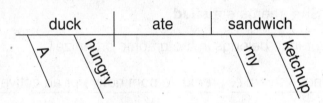 

Write details on the lines to complete each sentence. Then, on another sheet of paper, draw a graphic organizer for each sentence. Write each sentence on its organizer.

1. The _____ boy sings a _____ song.

2. The _____ bird ate a _____ worm.

3. _____ waves sank the _____ boat.

4. The _____ man cut a _____ watermelon.

W R I T E   A W A Y

Write details on the lines to complete each sentence. Then, on another sheet of paper, draw two graphic organizers and write your sentences in the organizers. Be sure to write each part in the correct place.

The _____ fire burned the _____ forest.

The _____ volcano flattened the _____ trees.

Name _____ Date _____

Expanding Sentences with Adjectives

How do you change a sad face into a happy face? All you have to do is change the adjective. **Adjectives** modify nouns and pronouns. Adjectives give details that help us tell one thing from another. With adjectives, we know the difference between a sunny sky and a cloudy sky. Adjectives add spice to writing. But as with most spices, you don't want to add too many. Choose your adjectives carefully.

- Look for sentences that do not give your ideas clearly.
- Think of adjectives that give a more exact picture.

The black ship topped **the crashing** waves.

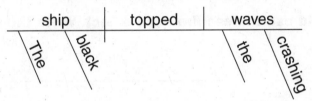

Add adjectives to expand each sentence. Write your new sentence on the line.

1. The lioness watches her cub. _____

2. Farmers grow crops. _____

3. The clerk found the shoes. _____

4. A car hit the wall. _____

5. The cup contains water. _____

WRITE AWAY

On another sheet of paper, write as many adjectives as you can that tell about each of these groups: colors, smells, tastes, sounds, textures.

Name _____ Date _____

Appeal to the Reader's Senses

Writing a good description is a special skill. You can make your reader see, smell, taste, hear, or feel just as you do. To be a good descriptive writer, you must appeal to the reader's senses. Many adjectives appeal to these senses. Choose adjectives carefully to match your purpose and voice.

- **sight:** orange, round, tiny, shiny
- **smell:** smoky, dusty, rotten
- **taste:** sour, salty, sweet, bitter
- **touch:** slick, sharp, cool, warm
- **hearing:** loud, quiet, squeaky

Choose adjectives that you could use to describe each object. Write the adjectives on the line.

1. an orange _____

2. a rainstorm _____

3. a worm _____

4. spaghetti _____

5. an orchestra _____

6. the last day of school _____

_____

WRITE AWAY

Write adjectives that tell about each sense. How many adjectives can you write for each sense?

sight _____

smell _____

taste _____

touch _____

hearing _____

Unit 2: Building Sentences
Core Skills Writing 6, SV 9781419039041

Expanding Sentences with Adverbs

The difference between doing something and doing something well is just an adverb. Adverbs modify verbs, adjectives, or other adverbs. Most adverbs tell how, when, where, or to what extent. Many adverbs that tell how end in *ly.*

> The snake **quickly** struck.   (how)
> We asked her **today.**   (when)
> Ducks quacked **everywhere.**   (where)
> The sky was **quite** beautiful.   (to what extent)

Adverbs are details that go under the main idea line in a graphic organizer. Write adverbs under the words they modify.

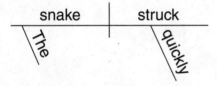

Write an adverb to expand each sentence. Then, on another sheet of paper, draw a graphic organizer for each sentence. Write each sentence on its organizer.

1. The man knocked _____.

2. He had been _____ waiting.

3. Mom _____ answered the door.

4. The man explained the problem _____.

5. He said he would return _____.

6. Mom was _____ angry.

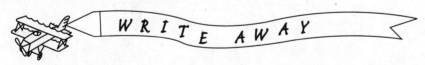

Most adverbs can be placed almost anywhere in a sentence. However, you should read your sentence aloud to hear which way sounds best. On another sheet of paper, write the adverb in parentheses in different places in the sentence. Read the sentences aloud. Which sounds best?

The small boat overturned in the water.   (clumsily)

Review: Modifiers

You can add details to a sentence by using modifiers such as adjectives and adverbs.

- An adjective modifies a noun or a pronoun.   **green** apple
- An adverb modifies a verb, an adjective, or another adverb.

    singing **happily**   **awfully** mean   **very** clearly

Modifiers are written under the main idea line in a graphic organizer. Write modifiers under the words they modify.

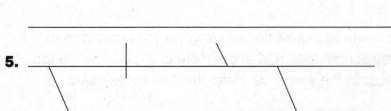

Write a sentence that will fit each graphic organizer below. Write your sentence on the organizer. Then write your sentence on the line.

1.

   _____

2.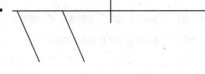

   _____

3.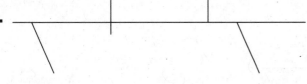

   _____

4. _____

   _____

5. _____

Name _____ Date _____

Clauses and Phrases

A **clause** is a group of related words that includes a subject and a predicate. **Independent clauses** can stand alone as complete sentences. Dependent clauses cannot.

Sharks swim.   (independent clause)

A **phrase** is a group of words that does not have a subject or a predicate. Phrases are not complete sentences. They do not tell a complete thought.

in the ocean

When you put an independent clause and a phrase together, you get an expanded complete sentence.

Sharks swim in the ocean.

Circle the independent clause in each sentence. Draw a line under the phrase.

1. Everyone should know about medical emergencies.

2. You can injure yourself in an accident.

3. Someone may be cut by a knife.

4. A person could break a bone in a fall.

5. In restaurants people sometimes choke.

6. You can help people with first aid.

7. The phone number for emergencies is 911.

8. Maybe you will be a doctor in the future.

W R I T E   A W A Y

On another sheet of paper, write seven short independent clauses and seven short phrases. Then cut them out. Mix and match the clauses and phrases. Can you make funny sentences?

Clauses and Phrases, page 2

In a graphic organizer, a phrase goes under the independent clause. The phrase "in the ocean" tells where, so it is an adverb. It is written under the verb in a sentence. Study the special lines the phrase is written on.

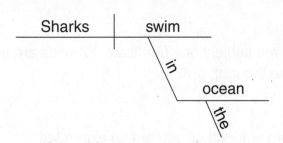

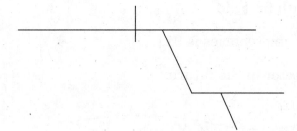

Add a clause or a phrase to complete each sentence. Then write the first sentence on the graphic organizer below. On another sheet of paper, draw graphic organizers for sentences 2.–5. Write each sentence on its organizer. Drawing an organizer is like working a puzzle.

1. We hiked _____.

2. The mountain peaks reached _____.

3. _____ down the river.

4. _____ in the snow.

5. We found an old cabin _____.

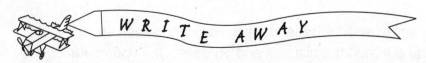

Remember adjectives and adverbs? They can be in sentences with phrases. On another sheet of paper, draw a graphic organizer for the sentence below. Write the sentence on the organizer.

Cool breezes blow gently through the valley.

Expanding Sentences with Prepositional Phrases

Many phrases you write will be **prepositional phrases.**

- Remember that a preposition shows the relation of a noun or pronoun to another word in a sentence.
- Some prepositions are *of, at, in, on, to, up, with,* and *from.*
- The noun or pronoun that follows the preposition is called the **object of the preposition.** If the object of the preposition is a pronoun, you must use an object pronoun.
- The preposition, the object of the preposition, and any other words form a prepositional phrase.
- Prepositional phrases can tell where, when, whose, why, how, or which.

> She saw a rare bird **in the forest.**   (where)
> I am an old friend **of his.**   (whose)
> She made the call **at once.**   (when or how)
> The dog **with sunglasses** ate the noodles.   (which)

Add a phrase to each sentence. Your phrase should tell where, when, whose, why, how, or which.

1. The old coat belonged _____.

2. They found their money _____.

3. Aunt Chia will return _____.

4. Sandy traveled _____.

5. The boy _____ waved to me.

6. My mother made snacks _____.

7. The ship ran aground _____.

8. The eagle landed _____.

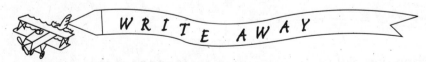

W R I T E   A W A Y

On another sheet of paper, write ten phrases that tell where your cat could hide in your house.   (under the chair)

Unit 2: Building Sentences
Core Skills Writing 6, SV 9781419039041

Expanding Sentences with Prepositional Phrases, page 2

Prepositional phrases can tell where, when, whose, why, or how. These kinds of prepositional phrases usually modify the predicate. They are known as **adverb phrases.** On a graphic organizer, each would be written under the verb.

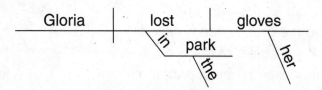

Prepositional phrases can also be used to tell which. This kind of prepositional phrase usually modifies the subject. They are known as **adjective phrases.** On a graphic organizer, the phrase would be written under the subject, object, or predicate nominative.

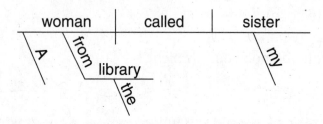

Write a prepositional phrase to complete each sentence. Look at the word in parentheses to tell what kind of prepositional phrase to write.

1. Jaxon journeyed _____. (where)

2. Margo went to the mall _____. (when)

3. The colorful cap belonged _____. (whose)

4. The band rehearsed _____. (why)

5. Carlos colored the column _____. (how)

6. The leader _____ gave a speech. (which)

On another sheet of paper, draw and complete a graphic organizer for each of the sentences above.

Expanding Sentences with Coordinate Conjunctions

Remember, a **conjunction** is a connective. It joins words or groups of words. **Coordinate conjunctions** are one important kind of conjunction. A coordinate conjunction joins two words, two phrases, or two clauses of equal rank. Some coordinate conjunctions are *and, or, but, yet, for, then,* and *however.*

> a boy **and** his dog   (*and* joins two nouns)
> safe **yet** fun   (*yet* joins two adjectives)
> in the morning **or** after breakfast   (*or* joins two prepositional phrases)
> Bart brought ice cream for lunch; **however,** it melted in his lunch box.   (*however* joins two independent clauses)

You can expand a sentence by using coordinate conjunctions. You can write compound subjects, compound predicates, compound modifiers, and compound sentences. Conjunctions are pretty handy, huh?

Write sentences using coordinate conjunctions. Use a coordinate conjunction to join the kinds of words named in parentheses.

1. (nouns) _____

2. (verbs) _____

3. (adjectives) _____

4. (adverbs) _____

5. (prepositional phrases) _____

_____

6. (independent clauses) _____

_____

W R I T E   A W A Y

Try to count the number of times you say or write *and* every day. On another sheet of paper, write a few sentences about how useful this word is to you. What would the world be like without it?

Compound Subjects and Compound Predicates

A **compound subject** has two or more simple subjects. The subjects are joined by a coordinate conjunction.

> **Gilbert** *and* **Shane** work for my brother.
> **Mia** *or* **Dewey** misplaced the materials.

A **compound predicate** has two or more simple predicates. The predicates are joined by a coordinate conjunction.

> You must **fish** *or* **cut bait.**
> Ed **ran, tripped,** *and* **stumbled.**

When you write a compound subject or compound predicate in a graphic organizer, you add the conjunction on a dotted line. The dotted line connects the two subjects or predicates.

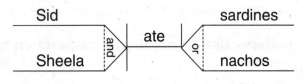

Write sentences with compound subjects and predicates as shown in parentheses. Then, on another sheet of paper, draw a graphic organizer for each sentence. Write the sentence on the graphic organizer.

1. (compound subject) _____

2. (compound predicate) _____

3. (compound subject and compound predicate) _____

_____

On another sheet of paper, write seven compound subjects and seven predicates. Cut them out. Mix and match the compound subjects and the predicates. Can you make silly sentences?

Name _____ Date _____

Agreement of Verbs and Compound Subjects

The subject of a sentence must agree in number with the verb.

- A singular subject must have a singular verb.

  My **sister lives** near the railroad tracks.

- A plural subject must have a plural verb.

- A compound subject that uses *and* is a plural subject. It requires a plural verb.

- A compound subject that uses *or* can be plural or singular. The verb agrees with the part of the compound subject closer to the verb.

  An apple *or* a banana **is** a healthy snack.   (singular)
  Raisins *or* an orange **is** a healthy snack.   (singular)
  An apple *or* carrots **are** a healthy snack.   (plural)

Write a verb to complete each sentence. Be sure your verb agrees with the subject.

1. Mice and crickets _____ in the field.

2. Cotton or silk _____ comfortable clothing.

3. Rats or bats _____ in the attic.

Write a compound subject to complete each sentence. Be sure your subject agrees with the verb.

4. A _____ or _____ taste good.

5. _____ or a _____ is in the envelope.

6. _____ or _____ make a good dessert.

On another sheet of paper, write five sentences. Each sentence should have a compound subject and a compound predicate. Be sure your verbs agree with your compound subject. Both verbs will be either singular or plural.

Name _____ Date _____

Subordinate Conjunctions

Subordinate conjunctions are another important kind of conjunction. A subordinate conjunction joins two clauses of unequal rank. A subordinate conjunction joins a **dependent clause** to an independent clause. The independent clause has a higher rank than the dependent clause. The main idea of the sentence goes in the independent clause. Some subordinate conjunctions are *as, because, before, since, when, where,* and *that.*

The sky was clear **before the lightning cracked.** ⟵ subordinate clause
Ivan was tardy **because his watch stopped.** ⟵ subordinate clause

Write a dependent clause to complete each sentence. Use the subordinate conjunction in the sentence.

1. Kenta was hungry because _____.

2. Maria had not been swimming since _____.

3. The wind stopped blowing before _____.

4. My sister was so happy that _____.

5. We can return the broken computer when _____.

6. The man was painting the wall where _____.

WRITE AWAY

Write five sentences that begin like the sentence below.

I like writing because _____.

_____

_____

_____

_____

_____

Unit 2: Building Sentences
Core Skills Writing 6, SV 9781419039041

Independent and Dependent Clauses

A subordinate conjunction joins two clauses of unequal rank. A subordinate conjunction joins a dependent clause to an independent clause. The main idea of the sentence goes in the independent clause.

```
independent          dependent
  clause               clause
 ⎧⎯⎯⎯⎯⎧⎯⎯⎯⎯⎯⎯⎯⎯⎯⎧
I was angry that they forgot my birthday.
```

An independent clause tells a complete thought. It may stand alone as a simple sentence. A dependent clause does not express a complete thought. It cannot stand alone.

Read each set of sentences. Circle the sentence with the more important information. Then use the two sentences to write a new sentence. Use a subordinate conjunction to connect an independent clause to a dependent clause.

1. Cleopatra ruled Egypt with her brother. He seized the throne.

_____

2. Cleopatra regained her throne. Julius Caesar helped her.

_____

3. Mark Antony ruled Rome. Julius Caesar died.

_____

4. Antony went to Egypt. He lived there for several years.

_____

W R I T E   A W A Y

Rewrite the two sentences below as one sentence containing an independent clause and a dependent clause. Use these subordinate conjunctions: *because, since, before, where, after, although.* Which of your new sentences makes the most sense?

People become more concerned about pollution. They learn about toxic waste.

Review: Connectives

Conjunctions and prepositions are connectives. Connectives join parts of a sentence.

- A coordinate conjunction connects words or groups of words of equal rank. Some coordinate conjunctions are *and, or, but,* and *yet.*
- A subordinate conjunction joins two clauses of unequal rank. Some subordinate conjunctions are *because, before, after, although,* and *that.*
- A preposition shows the relation of a noun or pronoun to another word in a sentence. Some prepositions are *of, at, in, on, to, up, by,* and *from.*
- The preposition, its object, and any other words make up a prepositional phrase.

A graphic organizer shows the role of connectives in the sentence.

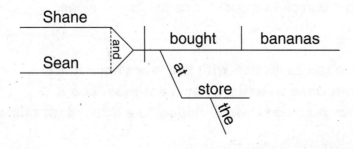

Write a sentence that will fit each graphic organizer below. Then write your sentence on the line. You can add lines to the graphic organizer if necessary.

1. _____

2. _____

Core Skills Writing 6, SV 9781419039041

Name _____ Date _____

Kinds of Sentences

There are four basic kinds of sentences: declarative, interrogative, imperative, and exclamatory.

- Use a **declarative sentence** to make a statement. You give information with this kind of sentence.
- Begin a declarative sentence with a capital letter. End it with a **period (.).**

  Africa is a continent.   Egypt touches the Mediterranean Sea.

- Use an **interrogative sentence** to ask a question. You get information with this kind of sentence.
- Begin an interrogative sentence with a capital letter. End it with a **question mark (?).**

  Is Pluto a planet?   How long is a journey to Mars?

Follow the directions to write sentences. Be sure to begin and end each sentence correctly.

1. Write a declarative sentence about France.

_____

2. Write an interrogative sentence about the French Revolution.

_____

3. Write a declarative sentence about the Atlantic Ocean.

_____

4. Write an interrogative sentence about the Arctic Ocean.

_____

5. Write a declarative sentence about South America.

_____

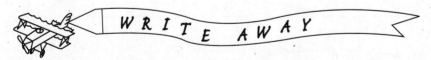

On another sheet of paper, write seven interrogative sentences. Then write seven declarative sentences to answer your questions.

Kinds of Sentences, page 2

There are four basic kinds of sentences: declarative, interrogative, imperative, and exclamatory.

- Use an **imperative sentence** to make a request or to give a command. You use this kind of sentence to make people do something.
- Begin an imperative sentence with a capital letter. End it with a period or an **exclamation mark (!).**
- The subject of an imperative sentence is the person to whom the request or command is given (*you*). The subject usually does not appear in the sentence. It is called an **understood subject.**

      (You) Please feed the cats.   (You) Get your feet off the table!

- Use an **exclamatory sentence** to show excitement or strong feeling. You use this kind of sentence when you are excited.
- Begin an exclamatory sentence with a capital letter. End it with an exclamation mark.

      A tornado is coming toward us!   I love exclamatory sentences!

Follow the directions to write sentences. Be sure to begin and end each sentence correctly.

1. Write an imperative sentence about reading a poem.

_____

2. Write an exclamatory sentence about a hurricane.

_____

3. Write an imperative sentence about sweeping the floor.

_____

4. Write an exclamatory sentence about a falling rock.

_____

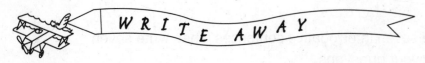

On another sheet of paper, write seven imperative sentences that give a command. Then write seven exclamatory sentences that respond to the commands.

End Punctuation

Be sure to use the correct punctuation at the end of your sentences.

- Use a **period (.)** at the end of a declarative sentence.
- Use a **question mark (?)** at the end of an interrogative sentence.
- Use a period or an **exclamation mark (!)** at the end of an imperative sentence.
- Use an exclamation mark at the end of an exclamatory sentence.

My pet hamster is missing.	Has anyone seen it?
Help us search for it.	It's in my bed!

Add the correct end punctuation for each sentence.

1. Have you ever lost your voice

2. What a strange feeling that is

3. You try to talk, but you can only squeak or croak

4. No one can understand you

Follow the directions to write sentences. Then tell what kind each sentence is.

5. Write a sentence that ends with a period.

_____

6. Write a sentence that ends with a question mark.

_____

7. Write a sentence that ends with an exclamation mark.

_____

8. Write a sentence that ends with a period.

_____

9. Write a sentence that ends with an exclamation mark.

_____

10. Write a sentence that ends with a period.

_____

Name _____   Date _____

Simple, Compound, and Complex Sentences

- A **simple sentence** contains only one complete thought. It contains only one independent clause.

  Diego was flying a kite.

- A **compound sentence** has two or more simple sentences. It has two or more complete thoughts. It contains two or more independent clauses.
- A compound sentence is joined by a coordinate conjunction such as *and, or,* or *but*. Use a **comma (,)** before a conjunction that joins two simple sentences.

  Diego was flying a kite, and then it crashed into a tree.

- A **complex sentence** contains one independent clause and one or more dependent clauses.

  The kite crashed into the tree because Diego did not tie the string tightly.

Rewrite each simple sentence to make it a compound or complex sentence.

1. The old man and the boy left the village.

_____

2. They traveled all day.

_____

3. Finally, they reached a beautiful lake.

_____

4. They set up a tent.

_____

5. The night sky was dark and full of stars.

_____

Write six simple sentences. Rewrite them as compound or complex sentences.

Unit 2: Building Sentences
Core Skills Writing 6, SV 9781419039041

Using Commas

- Use a **comma** before the word *and, but,* or *or* when two sentences are joined in a compound sentence.

   The second sun set, **and** a purple moon rose in the east.

- Use commas to separate three or more words in a **series**.

   The lone astronaut carried **a blanket, some matches, and a flashlight.**

- Use a comma to separate an introductory word or name from the rest of the sentence.

   Captain Spaceley, what kind of mess are you in now?
   Yes, I guess it does look bad.

Complete each compound sentence by adding a second sentence. Be sure to add a comma and a conjunction.

1. Spaceley trudged across the sandy surface _____

   _____.

2. Lightning flashed in the dark sky _____.

3. _____ and soon he fell asleep.

Complete each sentence by adding a series of three or more words. Be sure to add commas and a conjunction.

4. Spaceley felt _____ in the morning.

5. In the purple sky, Spaceley saw _____.

6. _____ chased him across the barren planet.

Complete each sentence by adding an introductory name or word. Be sure to add a comma.

7. _____ get off our planet!

8. _____ I'm leaving as soon as I can!

Name _____ Date _____

Combining Sentences

Too many short sentences are boring. You can gain sentence variety by changing the lengths of your sentences. Make your writing more interesting by combining sentences.

- Simple sentences with similar ideas can be combined.
- Join the sentences with a coordinate conjunction and a comma.
- Be sure the conjunction makes the meaning of the combined sentences clear. *And* shows addition, *but* shows difference, and *or* shows choice.

A crater can be formed by an explosion. A crater can be formed by a meteorite.
A crater can be formed by an explosion, **or** it can be formed by a meteorite.

Write a second sentence that is related to the first sentence. Then join the two sentences. Use the conjunction in ( ) to join the sentences. Make sure your sentence agrees with the meaning of the conjunction.

1. The meteorite suddenly rushed past Captain Spaceley. (but)

Second sentence: _____

Combined sentence: _____

_____

2. Captain Spaceley ran to the rim of the crater. (and)

Second sentence: _____

Combined sentence: _____

_____

3. Captain Spaceley could stay where he was. (or)

Second sentence: _____

Combined sentence: _____

_____

4. When will Captain Spaceley learn? (and)

Second sentence: _____

Combined sentence: _____

_____

Unit 2: Building Sentences
Core Skills Writing 6, SV 9781419039041

Combining Sentences with the Same Subject or Predicate

A good writer may choose to combine two or more sentences that have the same subject or predicate. The coordinate conjunctions *and, or,* and *but* are often used to combine sentence parts.

- When two sentences have the same predicate, the subjects can be combined. When you combine subjects, be sure you use the correct form of the verb.

   Marley likes adventures. Carley likes adventures.
   Marley *and* Carley like adventures.

- When two sentences have the same subject, the predicates can be combined.

   Marley stuck his head in the bucket. Marley peeked through the hole.
   Marley **stuck his head in the bucket *and* peeked through the hole.**

Rewrite this paragraph. Combine sentences with the same subjects or predicates to make them more interesting to read. You may change some words. Use another sheet of paper.

Carley looked down at the hole in the ground. Marley looked down at the hole in the ground. They couldn't see much. Marley scratched his head. Marley wondered what to do. Meanwhile, Carley ran to the house. Carley returned with a flashlight. Marley nodded at Carley. Carley nodded at Marley. Carley shined the light down the hole. Suddenly a red rabbit jumped from the hole. The red rabbit started to yell at them.

WRITE AWAY

Here's something just for fun. On another sheet of paper, continue the story of Marley, Carley, and the rabbit. First, write your story in short sentences. Then, read your story aloud to find sentences with subjects or predicates that you can combine. Rewrite the paragraph using the new combined sentences. Which version is better writing?

Name _____   Date _____

Review: Working with Sentences

You can make your writing better by using different kinds of sentences. You can make your writing more lively by combining sentences or parts of sentences.

Follow the directions to write sentences. Be sure to begin and end each sentence correctly.

1. Write a simple interrogative sentence about a current event.

_____

2. Write a compound declarative sentence about a strange place.

_____

3. Write a simple exclamatory sentence about your favorite season.

_____

4. Write a compound imperative sentence about cleaning your room.

_____

5. Form a compound sentence by writing a second sentence. Be sure to add a comma and a conjunction.

The bear awoke from its long sleep _____.

6. Write a simple declarative sentence that contains a series.

_____

7. Write a complex sentence that uses the subordinate conjunction *before*.

_____

_____

8. Combine the two short sentences into one longer sentence.
Erica started down the dark path. She stopped when she heard a strange noise.

_____

_____

Active and Passive Verbs

Strong verbs make writing livelier and more active. They keep your reader awake. Try this. Write a sentence and read it aloud. How does it sound? Does it make you fall asleep? Maybe you need stronger verbs. Let's test. What do you think of this sentence?

The winter **was** very cold.

The verb *was* is rather weak. *Was* is a **passive verb.** All of the *be* verbs *(is, are, was, were, am, be, been, being)* are passive. The sentence needs an **active verb.**

The winter cold **chilled** us to the bone.

Chilled is an **active verb.** We can see the action in our heads. We are more interested. Use active verbs to make your writing more interesting.

Rewrite each sentence. Change the passive verbs to active verbs. You may have to change the way the sentence is written.

1. Kayla was very mad.

_____

2. The spring weather was pleasant.

_____

3. The haiku was written by Jin.

_____

4. The students are reading about world history.

_____

5. I was happy that the test was done.

_____

On a sheet of paper, write five passive sentences. Then rewrite each using active verbs. Compare the two sets of sentences. How are they different? Which is better? Write your thoughts.

Verb Tense

Tense means "time." So, **verb tense** tells the time of the action or being.

- Use a **present tense verb** to tell what is happening now. The action is continuing.
- Use a **past tense verb** to tell what happened in the past. The action is completed.
- Use a **future tense verb** to tell what will happen in the future. The action has not yet begun.

They **dance** now.　　　They **danced** yesterday.　　　They **will dance** next week.
(present tense)　　　　　(past tense)　　　　　　　　　(future tense)

If you use the wrong verb tense, your reader will be lost in time. That's not good.

Write a verb to complete each sentence. Use clues in the sentence to write the correct verb tense.

1. Uncle Mike _____ in his shop every day.

2. Yesterday he _____ some bookcases.

3. He _____ to build some chairs tomorrow.

4. Mike _____ to work in his shop each day.

5. Candis sits and _____ the clouds.

6. She _____ the same kind of clouds yesterday.

7. Last night, the rain _____ for hours.

8. Perhaps it _____ again later tonight.

9. Augie _____ first base in tomorrow's game.

10. He _____ two home runs in last night's game.

W R I T E   A W A Y

Write a list of 15 verbs. Then make a chart with three columns. At the top of one column, write *present tense*. At the top of the second column, write *past tense*. At the top of the third column, write *future tense*. Write your 15 verbs in the correct place in the chart. Complete the chart by writing the correct tense of each verb in the columns.

Writing Descriptive Sentences

When you write a **descriptive sentence,** you give the reader details. Use specific details that tell who, what, when, where, and how. Your descriptive sentence should let the reader "see" the scene in his or her mind. The following sentence tells about the object, but the reader cannot "see" the scene.

The fountain is wonderful and spectacular.

This sentence needs more specific adjectives than "wonderful" and "spectacular." These adjectives don't really describe the object. Here's a better descriptive sentence.

The illuminated fountain sprayed cold water high into the night sky.

Good descriptive sentences use strong verbs and specific adjectives and adverbs.

Rewrite each sentence to make it more descriptive. Use strong verbs and specific adjectives or adverbs.

1. The fire in the fireplace was nice.

_____

2. The house was roomy and pleasant.

_____

3. The backyard was full of plants.

_____

4. A swing was in the backyard.

_____

5. The trees were good.

_____

WRITE AWAY

What is your favorite possession? On another sheet of paper, write five descriptive sentences about it. Use strong verbs and specific adjectives or adverbs in your sentences.

Writing Descriptive Sentences, page 2

Good description creates a mental picture for your readers. How do you create a mental picture? You use specific details. Adjectives are good for details. You want your words to control what your readers "see" in their minds. You must appeal to their senses. Think about your word choices. That's what good writers do.

The sweet, cold juice of the deep red watermelon tingled my tongue.

You want to describe your home for someone who has never been there. Write five adjectives for each sense. Remember, think about your choices.

Sight: _____

Smell: _____

Touch: _____

Sound: _____

Taste: _____

Choose the best adjective for each sense from your lists above. Use the five best adjectives to write a descriptive paragraph about your home. Use another sheet of paper if necessary. Remember, create a mental picture for your reader. Don't just write sentences listing the adjectives.

Best adjectives: _____

_____

_____

_____

_____

WRITE AWAY

Name _____ Date _____

Writing Descriptive Sentences, page 3

Strong adjectives are good for creating mental pictures. Adverbs are good, too. But strong verbs are better. Strong verbs can make your description livelier.

The earthquake **trembled** the city.

Write five active verbs that mean the same as the words given. Write only verbs. Do not use adverbs.

1. find _____

2. smell _____

3. hold with your hand _____

4. move unsteadily _____

5. jump _____

6. move quietly _____

Revise each sentence. Use a strong verb. Use strong adjectives. Make your writing clear and direct.

7. The snowball that was very large was rolling down the mountainside through the trees.

_____

8. The kids of different ages that were playing at the park were making many sounds.

_____

9. The sunrise was very beautiful.

_____

 W R I T E   A W A Y

On another sheet of paper, rewrite the sentence below five times. Replace the verb with a stronger verb in each sentence.

Trevor climbed up the cold, steep mountain.

59

Name _____ Date _____

Using Figurative Language

Writers sometimes use **figurative language** to compare unlike things. The words in figurative language don't really mean what they say. If a man is very hungry, he might say he could eat a horse. He doesn't really mean it, though. He is using figurative language.

- A **simile** compares two things by using *like* or *as*.

  The storm swept over the plains **like a giant mop.**
  The thick, green grass was **like carpet** under our feet.

- A **metaphor** compares two things by speaking of one thing as if it were another. A metaphor does not use *like* or *as*.

  The comedian was **a barrel of laughs.**
  A wave of laughter swept through the crowd.

Complete each simile or metaphor.

1. The orchestra drums rumbled like _____.

2. The moon was _____.

3. He was as slow as _____.

4. My room is _____.

5. Paying bills is like _____.

6. The cool breeze was like _____.

7. Our emotions are like _____.

8. Roger ran like _____.

W R I T E   A W A Y

Rewrite each sentence below. State the same idea but use a simile or metaphor.

Kayla was very funny.

_____

Hail fell on the roof.

_____

Name _____ Date _____

Using Figurative Language, page 2

When you use figurative language, you can create strong pictures in your reader's mind. You can create vivid word pictures by comparing two things that are not usually thought to be alike.

- **Personification** makes nonhuman things seem human. Objects, ideas, places, or animals may be given human qualities. They may perform human actions.

   The **flames ate hungrily** at the burning house.
   The **waves danced** along the shoreline.

Rewrite each sentence but do not use personification.

1. The sailboat danced gracefully past us.

_____

2. The computer devoured information all day long.

_____

3. The hikers left the meadow and were swallowed up by the forest.

_____

Rewrite each sentence but use personification to make it more interesting.

4. Fog covered the houses.

_____

5. The tree branches moved in the breeze.

_____

6. The clock showed midnight.

_____

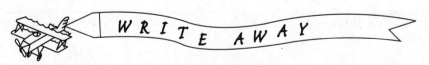
WRITE AWAY

On another sheet of paper, write sentences that personify these things.

   a rock   a snake   a door   a duck

Name _____   Date _____

Sentence Variety

Sentence variety makes your writing interesting. Sentences that begin the same way or have the same order are boring. There's a saying that "variety is the spice of life." Well, variety is the spice of writing, too. Let's look at some ways to spice up your writing.

- You can begin a sentence with an adjective or adverb.

  Sad were the voices at the funeral.
  Bravely the man fought the intruder.

- You can begin a sentence with a preposition or the object of the sentence.

  Around the bend a new surprise waited.
  Some problems I ignore.

- You can change the order of the subject and the verb. This is called **inverted order.**

  Flying in a balloon **was** Tanya's **dream.**
  In the sky **appeared rainbows.**

Follow the directions to write sentences. Be sure to begin and end each sentence correctly.

1. Write a sentence about rain that begins with an adjective.

_____

2. Write a sentence about quacking ducks that begins with a preposition.

_____

3. Write a sentence about eating food that begins with the object of the sentence.

_____

4. Write a sentence about an explorer that begins with an adverb.

_____

5. Write a sentence that uses inverted order.

_____

Sentence Lengths

You can also get variety by changing the lengths of the sentences you write.

- Short sentences tell about the main idea or present actions better.

  My pet **snake disappeared.**
  The **car zoomed** around the track.

- Longer sentences help to explain details better.

  The woman **in the blue dress** shouted **angrily at the two boys.**

- Compound sentences let you tell about two related ideas.

  Storm **waves crashed** against the shore, **and Adam hurriedly tied the boat** to the dock.

Follow the directions to write sentences. Be sure to begin and end each sentence correctly.

1. Write a short sentence that shows a main idea clearly.

   _____

2. Write a short sentence that shows a strong action.

   _____

3. Write a longer sentence with several details.

   _____

4. Write a longer compound sentence that tells about two related ideas.

   _____

   _____

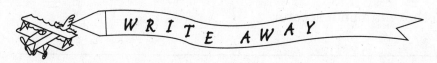

On another sheet of paper, practice writing the same idea in sentences of different lengths. Do the shorter or longer sentences help you express yourself better?

Sentence Errors: Fragments

A good sentence expresses a complete idea. It has a subject and a predicate. It uses correct punctuation. But sentence errors can make your writing unclear and confusing. You need to check your writing to be sure you do not have sentence errors.

One common error is the **sentence fragment.** A sentence fragment is only a part of a sentence. It is not a complete sentence. It does not tell a complete thought. You should remove fragments from your writing.

Went to a game at the park.   (fragment—no subject)
Sandy and the boy who hit the home run.   (fragment—no predicate)
At the end of the second inning.   (fragment—prepositional phrases)
When the ball rolled to the fence.   (fragment—dependent clause)
No one on the Gophers got a hit.   (complete sentence)

Rewrite each fragment to make it a complete sentence. If the group of words is a complete sentence already, write *not a fragment.*

1. Because the bus was leaving soon.

_____

2. Discovered some old bones in a cave.

_____

3. Through the storm, the truck rushed on.

_____

4. People travel to the moon.

_____

5. Many different types of birds at the zoo.

_____

6. The driver of the truck and another man on a scooter.

_____

7. When the leaves begin to fall in the autumn.

_____

Core Skills Writing 6, SV 9781419039041

Sentence Errors: Run-on Sentences

Another common error is the **run-on sentence.**

- A run-on sentence happens when you join two complete sentences without any punctuation. This error is also known as a **fused sentence.**
- To fix a run-on like this, join the two sentences with a comma and a coordinate conjunction.
- You can also use a period and write the run-on as two separate sentences.
- You can also join the two sentences with a subordinate conjunction. You must make one idea more important than the other idea.

> She asked for help I ignored her.   (run-on)
> She asked for help, **but** I ignored her.   (fixed)
> She asked for help. I ignored her.   (fixed)
> **Though** she asked for help, I ignored her.   (fixed)

Correct each run-on sentence. Write the new sentence or sentences on the line.

1. Aristotle lived in ancient Greece he became a great philosopher.

_____

_____

2. Plato was a famous philosopher Aristotle attended his school.

_____

3. Aristotle became famous himself many people studied his work.

_____

_____

4. Aristotle taught Alexander the Great Alexander became king of Macedonia.

_____

_____

5. Aristotle started his own school he received money from Alexander.

_____

_____

Sentence Errors: Run-on Sentences, page 2

- A run-on sentence also occurs when you join two complete sentences with only a comma. This error is also known as a **comma splice.**
- To fix a run-on like this, use a period and write the run-on sentence as two separate sentences.
- You can also join the two sentences with a comma and a coordinate conjunction.
- You can also join the two sentences with a subordinate conjunction. You must make one idea more important than the other idea.

He walked slowly on the way, he did not get home until dark.   (run-on)
He walked slowly on the way. He did not get home until dark.   (fixed)
He walked slowly on the way, **so** he did not get home until dark.   (fixed)
Because he walked slowly on the way, he did not get home until dark.   (fixed)

Correct each run-on sentence. Write the new sentence or sentences on the line.

1. Friction makes meteors incredibly hot, they burn up miles above Earth's surface.

_____

_____

2. Some large meteors do not burn up completely, they are called meteorites.

_____

_____

3. A meteorite exploded over Siberia, it created more than 200 craters.

_____

_____

4. A meteorite crashed there perhaps 50,000 years ago, it may have fallen earlier.

_____

_____

Building a Sentence

If you can see—not read, but see—your writing, you have a better idea of each part's role in the sentence. You can "see" the main idea of the sentence and the location of details. Seeing your writing can help you organize it better. Then you can build better sentences.

Writing is a process. Follow the steps below to build a better sentence.

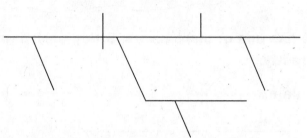

Step 1: First, write a main idea for the sentence: **Niki grows flowers.** You can write it on the main idea line of the graphic organizer.

Step 2: We could stop right there. We have a complete sentence. It's not a very informative sentence. Maybe we should add some details. Remember, everything that is not in the main idea of the sentence is a detail. Think of the questions a reader might ask. Write each new part on the graphic organizer.

What kind of flowers?   Niki grows **purple** flowers.

Where does she grow them?   Niki grows purple flowers **in her garden.**

What about Niki?   **Friendly** Niki grows purple flowers in her garden.

Now you have a detailed sentence. Your reader gets a much clearer mental image.

W R I T E   A W A Y

Use the process above to write three detailed sentences on another sheet of paper. Write a detail question, and then add the detail to the sentence. You can write about things in a garden, or you can use a topic of your choice. Then draw a graphic organizer for each sentence. Write each sentence in its organizer.

Self-Evaluation: What's Going On?

You've been studying hard, of course, and writing all kinds of interesting things. Have you learned anything? Do you think you are a better writer now? Do you know what a good sentence is? Well, on this page, you will get a chance to show what you've learned.

Each of the following sentences has one or more errors. Study each sentence. Then rewrite each sentence correctly.

1. Look at those too bears in thta airplain.

_____

2. Their flying just above the treetops in a blew biplane.

_____

3. Those to bears has two be crazy?

_____

4. Now their flying aobve the cotten clowds.

_____

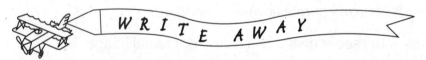

W R I T E   A W A Y

Take your time on this activity and do your best writing. First, on another sheet of paper, write three sentences that tell about something you really like. These sentences are your first draft. Write quickly and get your ideas on paper. Be sure your main idea is strong and clear.

Revise your sentences. Do the sentences say what you mean? Will your reader understand your meaning? Can the word choice be improved? Think about your sentences for five minutes. Read each one aloud once or twice. Then, rewrite each sentence three more times. Read each sentence aloud again as you are writing it. How does it sound? Is the punctuation correct? Add important details your reader will need to know.

OK, now choose the best version of each sentence. Write the three sentences in final form. Compare your final three sentences to the Self-Evaluation Checklist on page 120. Check each point that agrees with your writing. How good is your writing? On another sheet of paper, write three or four sentences that describe your writing style.

What Is a Paragraph?

A **paragraph** is a group of sentences that tells about one main idea. A good paragraph has unity, coherence, and emphasis. **Unity** means that every sentence in the paragraph supports the main idea. **Coherence** means that the parts of the paragraph have a logical order. **Emphasis** means that the important ideas are stressed, not minor or unnecessary ideas. A paragraph has three parts.

- The **topic sentence** tells the main idea of the paragraph.
- The **detail sentences** tell more about the main idea.
- The **concluding sentence** closes the paragraph. It restates the main idea and summarizes the information in the paragraph.

Read each paragraph below. How well does each paragraph tell about one main idea? Write a few sentences about each paragraph. Tell why it is or is not a good paragraph. Then, if you think the paragraph is weak, correct it and rewrite it on another sheet of paper.

1. In the 1800s, the struggle for women's rights began. Some people believed that women were not treated fairly or equally. Women were not allowed to vote. They could not get good jobs, such as being doctors or lawyers. Women who did have jobs earned much less than men with similar jobs. Many women began to speak out for equality.

_____

_____

_____

2. Sounds are measured in units called decibels. Decibels begin at 0 for sounds that a human with normal hearing would not be able to hear. Some people, like my grandfather, can't hear anything. He turns the TV up really loud, and then we have to yell to be heard. As sounds get louder, the number of decibels gets higher. At a certain point, sounds become so loud they are painful. Watching TV with my grandfather is a pain, believe me.

_____

_____

_____

Name _____   Date _____

What Is in a Paragraph?

A paragraph is a group of sentences about one main idea. The first sentence of the paragraph is **indented.** There are usually several sentences in a paragraph. Many paragraphs have five sentences. Try to avoid writing very long or very short paragraphs.

When you write a paragraph, you want it to have a logical order. A good paragraph has a certain movement. The information in the paragraph goes from

general   **to** →   specific   **to** →   general

- The **topic sentence** is general. It introduces the topic or main idea of the paragraph, but it does not give details. The topic sentence eases the reader into the paragraph.
- The **detail sentences** are specific. They give details about the topic of the paragraph. They tell who, what, when, where, how, and why.
- The **concluding sentence** is general. It restates the main idea and sums up the information in the paragraph. The concluding sentence eases the reader out of the paragraph.

➤ **Read the paragraph below. Then write sentences to answer each question.**

Luna was the Roman goddess of the moon. From her name come many words we use every day. From Luna we get *lunar,* which means "to shine" in Latin. In the past, many people believed that the light of the moon could influence human behavior. This influence was especially strong during a full moon. From those beliefs come *lunacy* and *lunatic,* words that describe irrational behavior. When people act goofy, they are often called *loony,* another word that comes from Luna. As you can see, words can have very interesting origins.

1. What is the topic of this paragraph?

_____

2. Write the topic sentence from the paragraph.

_____

3. Write a detail sentence from the paragraph.

_____

4. Write the concluding sentence from the paragraph.

_____

Name _____ Date _____

Writing a Topic Sentence

A **topic sentence** introduces the topic or main idea of a paragraph. It tells what all the other sentences in the paragraph are about. The topic sentence is usually the first sentence in a paragraph, but it does not have to be in that position. A topic sentence should have **focus**. Focus means you have narrowed down the topic. For example, you might have the general topic of money. You could focus on coin collecting.

Coin collecting is a popular hobby of many people. This hobby is also called numismatics. Many coin collectors hope they will find a rare coin and become rich. Others collect coins simply for enjoyment. After all, coin collecting is money in the bank.

Read each topic below. Then choose a focus for each topic. Write a topic sentence that you could use to write a paragraph about your topic.

1. Topic: volcanoes

   Focus: ___active volcanoes_____

   Topic sentence: ___Popocatepetl is a dangerous volcano near Mexico City.___

2. Topic: sports

   Focus: _____

   Topic sentence: _____

   _____

3. Topic: Asia

   Focus: _____

   Topic sentence: _____

   _____

W R I T E A W A Y

On another sheet of paper, write a paragraph using one of your topic sentences.

Unit 3: Building Paragraphs
Core Skills Writing 6, SV 9781419039041

Writing Detail Sentences

The body sentences in a paragraph are **detail sentences.** Detail sentences give facts or examples about the topic. Details tell who, what, when, where, how, and why. Detail sentences help the reader learn more about the topic.

Choose your details carefully. Don't put a detail in your paragraph just because you think of it. A good plan is to list all the details you can think of. Consider what the reader needs to know about the topic. Then choose the three details that best support the topic sentence. Include the details in three body sentences.

Coin collecting is a popular hobby of many people. **This hobby is also called numismatics. Many coin collectors hope they will find a rare coin and become rich. Others collect coins simply for enjoyment.** After all, coin collecting is money in the bank.

Complete the prewriting steps below. What does New Year's Day make you think of? Write some details. Then narrow your thoughts on New Year's Day to the given topic sentence.

Topic: New Year's Day

Details about New Year's Day: _____

_____

_____

Topic sentence (focus): New Year's Day is a time to think of the year behind and the one ahead.

Choose three best details from above for this topic sentence. Write three detail sentences that support the topic sentence.

_____

_____

_____

Writing a Concluding Sentence

A **concluding sentence** ends the paragraph. It restates the topic sentence in different words. It sums up the information in the paragraph. It can also explain what the information means. It may relate the information to the real world.

Imagine that your paragraph is a sandwich. The two slices of bread hold all the details inside—the turkey, the lettuce, the onion slices. The top slice of bread is the topic sentence. The bottom slice of bread is the concluding sentence. It is similar to the top slice but not exactly, just as the concluding sentence is like the topic sentence but not exactly. Read the paragraph about coin collecting again. Notice how the topic sentence and the concluding sentence are similar but not exactly alike. Use the Paragraph Structure Chart on page 124 to organize your ideas.

  Coin collecting is a popular hobby of many people. This hobby is also called numismatics. Many coin collectors hope they will find a rare coin and become rich. Others collect coins simply for enjoyment. **After all, coin collecting is money in the bank.**

What does the expression "money in the bank" mean? In what ways does a coin collection have value?

Read the paragraph below. Then write two possible concluding sentences for the paragraph.

  In all the stories I have read, I have found three kinds of heroes. The first kind succeeds by bold courage alone. The second type of hero wins by cleverness or wit. The third type is the hero who succeeds in spite of his or her foolishness or limitations.

Concluding sentence 1: _____

_____

Concluding sentence 2: _____

_____

Prewriting a Paragraph

Anything you want to do well takes practice. **Prewriting** is a step when you think about what you will write. Prewriting is sometimes called **brainstorming.** Prewriting has three main chores.

- Think about your topic and audience.
- Choose your details.
- Organize your ideas.

Prewriting is an important skill to practice. Prewriting can take place in the seconds before you write a sentence or in the weeks before a big research project is due. When you prewrite, you work on ideas and words in your mind more than on paper. The Prewriting Survey on pages 114 and 115 can help you with your prewriting chores.

You have an assignment to write a paragraph about your favorite person from history. Do some prewriting. Think about what you must write. Fill in the chart below to help you to prewrite.

Main goal of assignment: _____

My topic: _____

My focus: _____

Details I might include: _____

_____

_____

_____

W R I T E   A W A Y

Pretend that you must write a speech to introduce your favorite person in history. Write 25 nouns, verbs, adjectives, and adverbs you might use in your speech. Use another sheet of paper.

Name _____ Date _____

Voice

When you talk to others, they can tell how you feel by listening to your voice. In writing, **voice** is the way a writer "speaks" to the readers. Voice is how your writing sounds. The readers can "hear" how you feel about the topic. Think about the people who might read what you write. With your writing and the care you put into it, you can influence what they think and how they feel.

Your voice should fit your topic. To choose your voice for a topic, you must think of your audience. Your voice should also fit your audience.

What voice would you use to write about a friend moving away?

_____

What voice would you use to write about a party celebrating your team's victory?

_____

 Follow the directions.

1. Name a topic you could write about using a serious voice.

_____

2. Name a topic you could write about using a happy voice.

_____

3. Name a topic you could write about using an angry voice.

_____

4. Name a topic you could write about using a humorous voice.

_____

5. Name a topic you could write about using a sad voice.

_____

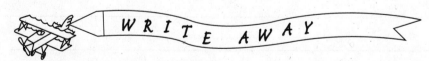

Pretend that your pet goat has run away. You must describe your feelings about the loss. Write a short paragraph about your feelings for your missing goat. Use a sad voice.

Unit 3: Building Paragraphs
Core Skills Writing 6, SV 9781419039041

Writing Pattern: Main Idea and Details

Writing patterns can help you organize your work. Choosing a pattern in the prewriting step will help you choose a writing form. For example, suppose you want to give information about a topic. You would probably choose the main idea and details pattern.

You already know about main idea and details. The main idea is the most important idea in the paragraph. The details tell who, what, when, where, how, and why about the main idea. Details give a clearer picture of the main idea. When you choose this pattern, the Main Idea and Details Web on page 121 can help you plan your work.

Look at your right hand. Suppose you have to describe it in an assignment. Use the Main Idea and Details Web on page 121 to write factual details about your right hand. Follow the directions to complete the organizer.

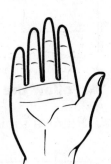

1. What is the topic or main idea? Write it in the center oval.

2. Which senses can you use to describe your right hand? How does it look? What color is it? How does it smell? How does it feel if you touch it? How does it taste? Write one detail in each circle. Draw more circles around the center oval if necessary.

3. What are some words that expand each detail? Write specific adjectives, adverbs, and nouns that you could use to write a paragraph.

_____

_____

Use the Main Idea and Details Web to write a paragraph that gives factual information about your right hand. Use another sheet of paper if necessary.

_____

_____

_____

_____

_____

Writing Pattern: Summary

When you write a **summary,** or **summarize,** you tell the most important details about something. You tell who, what, where, when, why, and how. You might use this writing pattern if you want to give your audience a short description of a book, story, or movie. You may need to summarize information for a research report.

- First, find the main idea of the selection. In a paragraph, the main idea is in the topic sentence.
- Then, decide on the key details about the topic. Don't tell all the details, but only the most important ones.
- Finally, write the summary. Identify the topic, the main idea, and the key details.

Remember to give the most important details so the audience understands the topic, but be brief. You can use the Summary Chart on page 122 to help you plan your work.

 Read the paragraph below. Then complete the Summary Chart on page 122. Follow the directions below to complete the chart.

Food is fuel for our bodies. The fuel value is measured in calories. An apple has about 75 calories, and a cup of peanuts has about 800 calories. You can see that peanuts furnish more heat and energy for the body than the apple does. Most children need about 2,000 calories a day. If more calories are taken in than the body needs, the body stores the extra food as fat. If not enough food is eaten, the body uses up fat since it must have fuel.

1. Write the important details from the paragraph on the left side of the box. Tell who, what, where, when, why, and how. You do not need to write complete sentences.

2. Use the details from the left side of the chart to write a summary. Write complete sentences. Do not include any extra information. Write as few sentences as you can, but be sure to include all the important details.

Unit 3: Building Paragraphs
Core Skills Writing 6, SV 9781419039041

Name _____ Date _____

Writing Pattern: Sequence of Events

Narratives and how-to directions use events in order. In both kinds of writing, you would choose a writing pattern that shows the **sequence,** or order, of events. Suppose you wanted to tell your friend how to make cookies. You would write the steps in order. You would use the sequence of events pattern to tell what to do first, next, and last.

Be sure to tell the action or steps in order. What if you were baking a pie? You would have a mess if the directions didn't tell you to put in the pie crust first.

When you choose this pattern, a sequence chart can help you plan your work. It helps you think about each step. You can plan which **time-order words** to use. Some time-order words are *first, next, then,* and *finally.* You can make your own chart like the one below. Add as many boxes and time-order words as you need.

First,	Next,	Then,	Finally,

Have you ever given someone directions to a place? Those directions use a sequence of steps. Give directions from your home to the nearest library. On another sheet of paper, draw a sequence chart to write the steps in order. Follow the directions below to complete the chart.

1. Which step do you do first? Write it in the first box.

2. Which step do you do last? Write it in the last box.

3. Which steps do you do in between? Write time-order words on the boxes. Then write the steps. Draw more boxes if necessary.

Use the sequence chart to write a paragraph. Give directions from your home to the nearest library. Use another sheet of paper if necessary.

_____

_____

_____

Unit 3: Building Paragraphs
Core Skills Writing 6, SV 9781419039041

Name _____ Date _____

Writing Pattern: Compare and Contrast

When you **compare** and **contrast**, you tell how two things are alike and different. If you compared a car to a bicycle, you could say that both are forms of transportation and both have wheels. To contrast the two machines, you could say that they have a different number of wheels and that the car has an engine but the bicycle doesn't. A car and a bicycle are alike and different at the same time.

This writing pattern is useful if you want to inform your readers how two things are similar or different. When you choose this pattern, a Venn diagram can help you plan your work. It helps you think about how the two items are related.

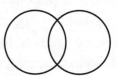

Compare and contrast two school subjects you study. Draw a bigger Venn diagram like the one above. Follow the directions below to complete the diagram.

1. Label each circle with the subject names. Write the name of the first subject above one circle. Write the name of the second subject above the other circle. Write *both* in the part where the circles overlap.

2. Look where the circles overlap. Write words that tell how the two subjects are alike in this space. For example, you might write *both use books*.

3. In the circle under the first subject, write words that describe that subject. They should tell how it is different from the second subject. Think about the information in the subject or what you do with that information.

4. In the circle under the second subject, write words that describe that subject. They should tell how it is different from the first subject.

Use the Venn diagram to write a paragraph. Compare and contrast the two school subjects. Use another sheet of paper if necessary.

_____

_____

_____

_____

_____

_____

Writing Pattern: Cause and Effect

A **cause** is why something happens. An **effect** is what happens. For example, a boy leaves a gate open and his dog gets out. In this example, the cause is the boy's carelessness. The effect is that the dog escapes.

The example above is a simple cause and effect event. However, one cause and effect pair can lead to a chain of cause and effect pairs. Think about the example above. Suppose the dog runs into the neighbor's yard and messes up the flowerbed. Then the neighbor yells at the dog, and the dog bites the neighbor. The neighbor goes to the doctor and takes the dog back home. All of these events occur because the boy forgot to close the gate. As you can see, each effect can lead to another cause. Each cause can lead to another effect.

This writing pattern is useful if you are telling why events happen. You must clearly state the cause and the effect so that a reader can understand why and what about an event. You can use the Cause and Effect Chart on page 123 to help you plan your work.

Think about a time you were late arriving somewhere. What caused you to be late? What were the effects of your being late? Use the Cause and Effect Chart on page 123 to explain the details. Follow the directions below to complete the chart.

1. Write the cause. Use exact nouns and verbs to explain the details.

2. Write the effect, or what happened. Use sense words so that the audience can "see" the effect.

Use the Cause and Effect Chart to write a paragraph. Tell about the time you were late. Use another sheet of paper if necessary.

_____

_____

_____

_____

_____

_____

_____

Writing Pattern: Problem and Solution

A **problem** is something that is wrong. It needs to be fixed. A **solution** is the way to fix the problem. The problem and solution writing pattern is useful to get the audience to agree with your solution. It can also be used to explain something that is a problem. For example, you might discuss how poverty is a big problem in this country and in the world. You could offer a solution to this problem.

When you use this pattern, be sure that the audience understands the problem. Identify the problem directly. Give examples and details that are clear and specific. Identify the solution directly. Explain why the solution works. When you choose this pattern, the Problem and Solution Chart on page 123 can help you plan your work.

Think about something that is a problem in the world today. Use the Problem and Solution Chart on page 123 to list the details. Follow the directions below to complete the chart.

1. Identify the problem directly. Give an example and list at least three details about the problem.

2. Identify the solution directly. Be specific. Tell why the solution would work.

Use the Problem and Solution Chart to write a paragraph. Identify a problem in your city and give your solution. Use another sheet of paper if necessary.

_____

_____

_____

_____

_____

_____

_____

_____

Keeping to the Topic

A paragraph should have unity. That means all the parts work together to tell about one main idea. One way to get unity is to keep to the topic. Be sure your paragraph doesn't contain **unnecessary information.**

Pretend that you and four friends are sitting at a table. You're eating lunch, and everyone is happy to be together. The group is like a good paragraph. You announce the topic of conversation: "Did you hear about the trouble at the mall?" (You're the topic sentence.) Three of your friends give details about the trouble. (They're the body sentences.) The fifth friend just nods and agrees with everyone. (He's the concluding sentence.)

Then your dad sits down at your table. He doesn't know anything about the topic. Your dad is like unnecessary information in a paragraph. It doesn't belong with the other information. When you write a paragraph, keep to the topic and remove details that do not support the main idea.

Read each paragraph carefully. Mark out the unnecessary information in the paragraph. Then write why the information is not needed.

1.   Cattle ranchers use brands to mark their cattle. Cattle can roam a long way. They can get mixed with cattle from another ranch. Cattle are not very smart animals, and they often moo too loud. The custom of marking calves with the owner's brand is common. Cowhands rope and brand the calves. The cowhands ride horses, too. After the branding, the calves return to their mothers.

_____

_____

2.   No harbor is complete without buoys. Buoys are floating objects that help sailors and boaters steer safely through dangerous waters near shore. Some buoys show that the water is too shallow for boats. Shallow water is good for swimming, though. Other buoys warn about rocks or mark the path a boat should follow. Buoys may have bells, whistles, or flashing lights. The main purpose of buoys is to keep boaters safe.

_____

_____

Revising

You must write so other people can understand your meaning. Maybe you can read what you have written and know what it means. Will your reader be able to understand it, too? Will your reader gain a mental picture of your meaning? That's where revising comes in. **Revising** means "seeing again."

To revise, pretend that you are reading someone else's writing. Then read what you have written. Read it aloud. You want the writing to seem new and fresh to you. Ask yourself some questions about what you have read.

- Is the writing clear and direct?
- Are the sentences complete ideas?
- Are the verbs active?
- Are the adjectives and adverbs clear and exact?
- Do the conjunctions show the correct meaning?
- Does the paragraph make sense?

The last question is probably the most important one. If you can't understand what you wrote, your reader won't, either. You have to revise the writing until it makes sense. Revising means you must rewrite.

Read the following paragraph. It is not very well written. Revise the paragraph. To revise, you must do more than correct grammar errors. You can add details and change sentences. You must improve the writing and make it clearer for the reader. Use another sheet of paper if necessary.

I remember going camping in the woods last year. We set up the tent and went to sleep. The next day we did some stuff. The next day we came home. It was one of the best times I ever had.

_____

_____

_____

_____

_____

_____

_____

Proofreading a Paragraph

Revising deals with improving the content of your paragraph. **Proofreading** deals with correcting your writing. When you proofread, you look for errors you have made. When you **edit,** you correct those errors. To be a good proofreader, look for one kind of error at a time.

- capitalization
- spelling
- punctuation
- grammar

An error-free paragraph is much easier to read. Complete the Proofreading Checklist on page 118. Use the chart of Proofreading Marks on page 119 to help you to edit your writing.

 Proofread the following paragraph. Pay attention to the kinds of errors listed above. Use the Proofreading Marks on page 119 to mark the errors. You should find at least 15 errors. Then write the edited paragraph below. Use another sheet of paper if necessary.

Can you imagine an animal that seams to be part mammal? Part reptile, and part bird? If you succeed, you will probly imagine an aminal like the platypus. In appeerance, the platypus most closely resembles a duck like a duck, it has a bill it also has webbed feet, fur, and a flat tale like a beaver's. Most mammills are warm-blooded Their temperature remains the same regardless of the temperture. Of their surroundings. A platypus is cold-blooded like a reptile, its body temperature changes with the temperture of it's surroundings.

_____

_____

_____

_____

Publishing

Once you have revised and edited your writing, you are ready to **publish** it. *Publish* means "to make public." In other words, you share your writing with others.

When you finish editing, write your final draft. Your final draft should be neatly written or typed. It should be free of errors. It should be the best you can write.

- Make a title page for your work.
- Think of a great title. Focus on words that you have used in your writing.
- Add pictures that might help to explain your topic.
- Use charts or bullets if needed to help your reader understand your topic.

If you have done your best, the publishing part should be the most fun in writing.

 Pretend that you have just finished a report on the platypus. Make a title page for your report. Include a title and some pictures.

Name _____ Date _____

Self-Evaluation: What's Going On?

In writing, there are two kinds of eyes—the writer's eyes and the reader's eyes. When you write, you use the writer's eyes. You see the words you have written through the writer's eyes. When you read someone else's writing, you use the reader's eyes.

A good writer has both kinds of eyes. The writer uses the writer's eyes while writing. Then, to revise, the writer uses the reader's eyes.

A good writer can tell how good his or her writing is. Self-evaluation can help you tell how good a writer you are.

 Write a paragraph below. Use another sheet of paper if necessary. You can write about your favorite place, your favorite memory, or a topic of your choice. Be sure to include a topic sentence, detail sentences, and a concluding sentence. Do your best writing.

Use the Self-Evaluation Checklist on page 120 to compare your paragraph to the checklist points. Check each point that agrees with your opinion of your writing. How good is your writing? What are the strengths and weaknesses of your writing? Do you have good control of the writing conventions? Do you have good word choice and sentence variety? Is your writing voice clear? What can you do to improve your writing? On another sheet of paper, write a paragraph that describes your writing style. Then write a paragraph that tells how you can improve your writing.

_____

_____

_____

_____

_____

_____

_____

_____

_____

_____

Unit 3: Building Paragraphs
Core Skills Writing 6, SV 9781419039041

Writing a Descriptive Paragraph: Person

When you **describe,** you paint a picture using words. You want the reader to "see" the thing you are describing. In fact, a good description lets the reader see, feel, hear, taste, or smell the thing. When you describe, you want to appeal to the reader's senses. The reader should feel as if he or she is with you examining the thing. Use vivid, concrete images. A concrete image is one that you can see in your mind, such as a blue dog. Remember to use your writing voice when you describe. You can describe persons, places, or things.

- When you describe a person, give unique details about the person.
- Most people have two ears, a nose, two arms, and so on. So you don't really have to deal with common details.
- First, give an overall view. Then, give specific details.

Rick had been a farmer all his life. He looked like a farmer, and he smelled of hay and horses. He wore faded blue overalls and a straw hat. He stood tall, straight, and thick. His hands were stumpy and rough. His face, clean shaven, had thin red lines crossing his cheeks, and his glasses sat square on his nose. You could tell he had lived a hard life, but his small grin suggested he enjoyed the life he had chosen.

First, choose a person to describe. Write a list of details you might use to describe that person. Remember to use unique details. Appeal to the reader's senses with your details. Use concrete images. Then, on another sheet of paper, write a paragraph describing that person.

Person I will describe: _____

Descriptive details I will use: _____

_____

_____

_____

_____

Writing a Descriptive Paragraph: Place

When you write a descriptive paragraph, write a topic sentence that tells what you are describing. Add detail sentences that give exact information about your topic. Use lively and colorful words to describe the topic. Remember to use concrete images. Paint a clear picture for your reader with the words you choose.

When you describe a place, give details that make the readers feel as if they are there.

- Group details in a way that makes sense.
- Provide a point of view from which to describe the place.
- You can also lead the reader through the place. Use movements such as front to back, top to bottom, or outside to inside.
- Try to give an emotional sense of the place. Use your writing voice.
- Be sure your topic sentence names the place you are describing.

When I was young, I loved my grandma's barn. I would open the creaky wooden door and enter another world. Tiny specks of dust floated in the strips of sunlight that slipped through the cracks in the boards. Smells came from everywhere—the smells of oats, of hay, of dust, of cows, and of manure. Heavy iron tools hung on the walls, tools used to shoe horses or farm the land. I would climb into the hay loft and look out over the countryside, and I felt like some explorer spying undiscovered lands. My grandma's barn is gone now, and I miss it very much.

> **Think of a place to describe. Then complete the graphic organizer below. Write the place in the circle. Write descriptive details on the lines. Use the graphic organizer to write a descriptive paragraph on another sheet of paper. Try to use movements that lead your reader around.**

_____

_____

_____

Writing a Descriptive Paragraph: Thing

Remember that a description paints a picture in words. Concrete images help your reader to see, hear, feel, smell, and taste what you are describing. Use colorful and exact adjectives as you describe. Use lively and active verbs, too.

When you describe a thing, identify it in your topic sentence.

- Use sensory words as you describe.
- Pretend that your reader is looking over your shoulder.
- Will your reader experience the thing as you do?

   Gulls are long-winged birds. Their bodies may be 11 to 30 inches long. But a gull's wingspan, or the length of its wings from tip to tip, may be more than 5 feet long. Most adult gulls have gray backs and white breasts. They may have black feathers on their wing tips. Most gulls have stocky bodies and square tails. If you have ever been to the beach, then surely you have seen lots of gulls.

Think of a thing to describe. It should be small, such as something you can hold in your hand. Then write a rough draft of your description. Name your thing in the topic sentence. Be sure to include sensory words. Try to describe only the details you can observe. Don't tell where it came from or what it can do. Give only physical details: what it looks or feels like, how it sounds or smells or tastes. Use another sheet of paper if necessary.

_____

_____

_____

_____

_____

Now revise your description. Have you painted a clear picture with your words? Are your verbs lively and active? After you revise, write your description again. This time, do not use these verbs: *is, are, was, were, am, be, been,* or *being.* Don't use any contractions containing these words either. Write your revision on another sheet of paper.

Writing a Narrative Paragraph

When you **narrate,** you tell about a **sequence** of events. Often the sequence tells what happens in a story. A story is also known as a **narrative.** The narrative can be fact or fiction. A narrative should have a beginning, a middle, and an ending. To write a narrative paragraph, follow these steps.

- Write an interesting beginning. Present your main **character** and the **setting.** The setting is when and where the narrative takes place. Introduce the character's problem.
- Tell about a problem the main character has to solve in the middle. Tell what happens in order. Use sensory details to make your story more realistic.
- Write an ending. Tell how the problem is solved. This is also called the **outcome.**
- Give your narrative a title.

Lost

The trail ended suddenly, but Leeza wanted to see what lay just over the ridge. Now she had lost sight of the trail, and Leeza had to admit that she was lost. Even worse, the sky was turning dark, and thunder began to rumble. Leeza felt like crying, but what good would that do? She had to decide whether to go forward or backtrack to try to find the trail. She chose to backtrack, because at least she thought she knew where she had come from. As she was scrambling through the underbrush, large drops of rain began to fall. The drops stung her skin and clouded her eyes. Now she would never find the trail. Suddenly, though, over the roar of the storm, she heard her father's voice calling for her. Leeza called out, and she tried to run, but she slipped and fell in the mud. She struggled to stand. Just then, a hand reached down to help her. Her father had found her. Leeza vowed never to leave the trail again.

Write a short narrative like the story of Leeza. Tell about a character who does something he or she should not do. First, introduce the narrative with a general statement. Then, give specific details to tell what happens in the narrative. When the events have ended, give a general statement about the outcome. Use another sheet of paper. Draw a picture to illustrate your narrative.

Name _____ Date _____

Personal Narrative

A **personal narrative** is a story about something you have done. Include your feelings and your writing voice in your personal narrative. The purpose of a personal narrative is to tell about you.

- Write from your point of view. Use words such as *I, me,* and *my* to tell your story.
- Organize the events into beginning, middle, and ending.
- Write an interesting beginning that "grabs" your readers.
- Give details in the middle that help the reader understand what is happening.
- Write the ending from your point of view.
- Remember to use your writing voice to tell the story. Include your personal feelings.

Summer Days

I remember fondly summer days I spent at my aunt's house. On washdays my cousins and I would play among my uncle's work shirts hanging on the line. The breeze would billow the shirts, and we pretended we were pirates sailing across the blue ocean. Sometimes my aunt mixed flakes of soap with a wire whip into a bowl of warm water. Then my cousins and I dipped empty thread spools into the solution and blew bubbles all around the yard. Sometimes the bubbles would pop in midair or on the green spikes of grass. We pretended to be great hunters and tied raw bacon on a string to lure crawfish from their muddy homes. I wish I could spend days like those again.

 Write a personal narrative paragraph about your memories of summer days. Be sure to have a beginning, a middle, and an ending in your narrative. Remember to indent the first line of your paragraph. Use another sheet of paper. Draw a picture to illustrate your narrative.

Dialogue

A narrative usually includes characters. Characters are real or made-up people or animals. They act in the events. Characters usually speak in narratives, too. What they say is called **dialogue.** When you write dialogue, you must follow some rules.

- **Place quotation marks (" ")** before and after the speaker's exact words.
- Use a comma to separate dialogue from the rest of the sentence unless a question mark or exclamation mark is needed. Any necessary comma or period goes inside the quotation marks.
- If dialogue is interrupted by other words, place quotation marks around the spoken words only.
- Begin a new paragraph each time the speaker changes.
- Be sure the dialogue sounds like real people talking. Avoid long speeches.
- Use the dialogue to tell what happens.

Lady President

Emma did not know if she was dreaming or awake. Somehow, she found herself in the Oval Office, and the President of the United States was asking her questions.

"Now, Emma," the President said, "how do we solve world hunger?"

"Well," she said, "I think we should give everyone enough to eat."

"Why, that's a good idea," the President said. "Why didn't I think of that? And what can we do about the war?"

"I think we should just tell everyone to stop fighting," Emma advised.

"Another good solution," the President said. "Maybe you should be sitting in this chair instead of me."

"Probably," Emma said, and then she awoke to her dog licking her face. She jumped out of bed, remembering she had a government test that day.

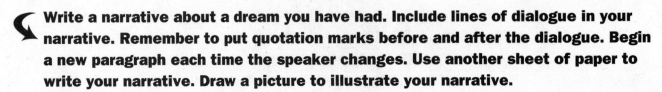

Write a narrative about a dream you have had. Include lines of dialogue in your narrative. Remember to put quotation marks before and after the dialogue. Begin a new paragraph each time the speaker changes. Use another sheet of paper to write your narrative. Draw a picture to illustrate your narrative.

Writing a Comparison and Contrast Paragraph

In a **comparison and contrast paragraph,** a writer shows how two people, places, things, or ideas are alike or different. You can also write paragraphs that only compare or contrast two things.

To **compare** means to show how two things are similar. To **contrast** means to show how two things are different.

People can live in both houses and apartments.   (compare)
Houses are separate structures, but apartments are in a building with other
    apartments.   (contrast)

For a good comparison and contrast, you should have only two items. You should write at least three ways the two items are similar or different.

**Read the comparison and contrast paragraph below. Then answer the questions.
Write complete sentences.**

Shelley's new house was similar to her old house in some ways, but it was different, too.
Like her old house, the new house had three bedrooms. Both houses had two bathrooms. They
both had a fireplace in the living room, and each house had a separate dining room. But the
new house looked and felt different from the old house. The old house was almost 100 years
old, but the new house had just been built. Unlike the old two-story house, the new house had
only one level. The old house had shiny hardwood floors, but the new house had wall-to-wall
carpet. Shelley did not know if she liked this new house as much as her old house.

1. What is the topic sentence of the comparison and contrast paragraph?

_____

_____

2. What are three ways the two houses are similar?

_____

_____

3. What are three ways the two houses are different?

_____

_____

Name _____ Date _____

Planning the Comparison and Contrast Paragraph

Here are some ways to write a good comparison and contrast paragraph.

- Think about your two items. Remember, do your prewriting to make your writing easier.
- Decide how the two items are similar. Decide how they are different. Choose at least three important similarities and differences.
- Write a topic sentence that tells that the two items are similar and different.
- Explain how the two items are alike. Explain how they are different. Give examples.
- Write a concluding sentence that summarizes the similarities and differences or gives a reaction to them.

Choose two items you want to compare and contrast. If you can't think of anything, compare and contrast kites and balloons. Draw a large Venn diagram like the one at the right. Follow the directions to complete the Venn diagram. Then use the Venn diagram to write a comparison and contrast paragraph on another sheet of paper.

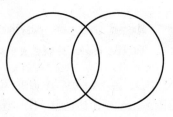

1. Label each circle with an item name. Where the circles overlap, write *Both*.

2. In the Both space, write words that tell how the two items are alike.

3. In the first circle, write words that describe the first item. They should tell how it is different from the second item. Think about shape, size, and use.

4. In the second circle, write words that describe the second item. They should tell how it is different from the first item.

Unit 4: Writing Forms
Core Skills Writing 6, SV 9781419039041

Writing a Definition Paragraph

In a **definition paragraph,** a writer answers the question "What is it?" about an object, a quality, or an idea. The definition is more than what the dictionary might say. This definition may be extended to include the writer's feelings about the topic.

- In the topic sentence, name the object, quality, or idea that will be defined.
- Give a clear definition for the topic.
- Use specific examples to support your definition in the detail sentences.
- Show how the definition can be applied to or distinguished from another idea.

I believe that the word <u>home</u> means more than just a place to live. My family had to leave our home in Berlin because we could no longer be safe there. We traveled on trains, stayed in hotels, and even slept in barns. Each of these places was home for us because we were together. Then we found a vacant house in Paris. It soon became our home because it provided us with peace, security, and comfort. The old saying is true: "Home is where the heart is."

Complete the graphic organizer with words you would use to define the word <u>family</u>. Then write a paragraph that explains your definition of <u>family</u>. Use another sheet of paper if necessary.

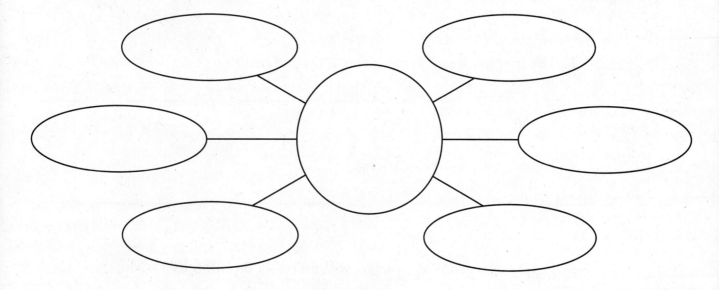

_____

_____

_____

Core Skills Writing 6, SV 9781419039041

Writing an Information Paragraph

An **information paragraph** tells facts about one topic. You know the difference between facts and opinions. **Facts** can be proved. **Opinions** are just somebody's ideas. Opinions usually can't be proved.

Fact: The largest shark is the whale shark, which can grow to 40 feet long.
Opinion: I think sharks are scary.

When you write an information paragraph, include only facts. Do not include opinions.

Write *fact* or *opinion* to identify each statement. Then tell why you think it is a fact or an opinion. Should it be included in an information paragraph?

_____ **1.** People should not go fishing for sharks.

_____

Include? _____

_____ **2.** The smallest shark is the pygmy dogfish, which can be only 5 inches long.

_____

Include? _____

_____ **3.** The hammerhead shark has a T-shaped head.

_____

Include? _____

_____ **4.** Hammerhead sharks are ugly.

_____

Include? _____

_____ **5.** People who swim at beaches will probably be eaten by sharks.

_____

Include? _____

Writing an Information Paragraph, page 2

An information paragraph can give facts about a topic. It can also tell how to do something or how something is done. To write an information paragraph, choose one topic. What will you write about that topic? You need a main idea. Suppose you are going to write about the topic of insects. What will your main idea be? What is your focus? You can write many things about insects. In an information paragraph, you need to develop one main idea about insects. Then you will give details about your main idea.

Topic: insects
Main idea (focus): Insects can be eaten for food.
Details:

   Insects are a common food in some parts of the world.
   In the United States, insects are sometimes sold in cans.
   Termite grubs are fried and eaten in some countries.
   Bees and ants may be roasted in oil.
   Caterpillars and other insects may be covered with chocolate.

Choose one of the topics in the box. Then complete the graphic organizer. What can you write about the topic? What will your main idea be? What facts do you know about the topic?

| hurricanes | bridges | the sun | doves |

Topic: _____

Main idea:

Detail 1:

Detail 2:

Detail 3:

Detail 4:

Writing an Information Paragraph, page 3

To write a good information paragraph:

- Choose one topic to write about.
- Write a topic sentence that tells your main idea about the topic.
- Write at least three detail sentences that tell facts about the main idea.
- Your details should tell who, what, when, where, how, or why.
- Be sure your facts are correct. Do not use opinions.
- Think of a title for your information paragraph.

You usually have to read about your topic to gather facts. When you read, think about the facts you are learning. Then write those facts in your own words. Do not just copy them from the place you are reading them. Use your own words. You should also tell about your **source,** or where you read the facts.

Use your graphic organizer from page 97 to write an information paragraph about your topic. If you read about your topic somewhere, write the name of your source. Use another sheet of paper if necessary.

Title: _____

Source: _____

_____

_____

_____

_____

_____

_____

_____

_____

_____

_____

_____

_____

Writing a Persuasive Paragraph

A **persuasive paragraph** tries to make the reader do something. You may want the reader to buy a particular product. You may want the reader to think or behave a certain way. You may want the reader to accept one side of an issue. An **issue** is an idea that people disagree about. For example, recycling can be an issue. Should people recycle more?

Each issue has two sides—pro and con. Pro is for, and con is against. State your side of the issue clearly in a **claim.** A claim is a statement telling which side of the issue you support.

> **Pro:** People need to recycle more.
> **Con:** People do not need to recycle more.

Then you give support. Write three detail sentences supporting your side of the issue. Order your support from weakest point to strongest point.

> People need to recycle more so more trash is not created.
> People need to recycle more because recycling saves energy.
> People need to recycle more because recycling saves natural resources.

Read the issue and the claim for the pro side. Write three support sentences for the pro side. Then write a con claim and three support sentences. Use another sheet of paper if necessary.

Issue: Should students be required to take standardized tests?

Pro claim: _Students should be required to take standardized tests._

Support sentences: _____

_____

Con claim: _____

Support sentences: _____

_____

Unit 4: Writing Forms
Core Skills Writing 6, SV 9781419039041

Writing a Persuasive Paragraph, page 2

When you persuade, you must think about your voice and your audience. You are trying to convince your readers. So you must choose your words carefully. Think about the audience you are trying to convince. What do those readers care about? How can you persuade those readers? Remember, you don't have to convince people that already agree with you. You can appeal to your readers in three ways.

Personal appeal: Talk to your readers directly. Use words such as *I, me,* and *my* to write your persuasion. Call the readers *you.* Make the readers like and trust you. Use your nicest writer's voice.

> I truly believe this is the best way to end world hunger.

Emotional appeal: Play with your readers' emotions. Appeal to your readers' likes, dislikes, and fears.

> If you buy this product, you will be like a movie star.

Logical appeal: Use facts and numbers to persuade the reader. When you have real data to support your view, it will have a stronger effect on the reader.

> A recent study suggests that people's bad eating habits begin before age 2.

Use the same issue about standardized testing. Choose which side of the issue you support. Write a personal appeal to support your claim about standardized testing. Then write an emotional appeal and a logical appeal to support your claim. Use another piece of paper if necessary.

Issue: Should students be required to take standardized tests?

Personal appeal: _____

_____

Emotional appeal: _____

_____

Logical appeal: _____

_____

Writing a Persuasive Paragraph, page 3

Remember, your purpose in a persuasive paragraph is to make your readers agree with you. To write a good persuasive paragraph:

- Tell your claim clearly.
- Think about which appeals will work with your audience.
- Use your three strongest support points.
- Give your weakest support point first and your strongest point last.
- A good concluding sentence helps a persuasive paragraph. Restate your claim and explain why it is true.

   In this age of fuel shortages, air travel should be greatly cut back. Of all the kinds of modern transportation, air travel is the least efficient. The Center for Transportation Research recently measured the efficiency of various methods of travel. They learned that while a jetliner averages only 26.4 passenger miles per gallon of fuel, the automobile averages 41.3, the diesel train 41.9, and the bus a spectacular 144.0! So, for efficiency's sake, we should all start thinking <u>bus stop</u> instead of <u>airport</u>!

Choose one side of the issue about testing on page 99. Use your claim, your appeals, and your support points to write a persuasive paragraph about standardized testing. Be sure your claim is clear. Order your support points from weakest to strongest. Talk directly to your reader. Use another sheet of paper if necessary.

_____

_____

_____

_____

_____

_____

_____

_____

Core Skills Writing 6, SV 9781419039041

Name _____ Date _____

Writing a Literary Response

Sometimes you may be asked to write a **literary response.** You will have to read a story or poem and then tell your ideas about the selection. In a literary response, you must do more than list the facts of the story or poem. The facts would be the names of characters, where and when the story or poem takes place, and the events that occur.

- You may have to identify the main character of the story or poem.
- You may have to tell why a character does something instead of what the character does.
- You may have to identify the main conflict of the story.
- You may have to explain the main idea of the story.

In a literary response, you will usually have to think more about *why* than about *what*.

Read the poem below. Then answer the questions. Write complete sentences. One answer is done for you.

The quiet night
Gentle breathing of branches.
The sun creeps
Glinting edges of hilltops.
A crow calls
Shrill salute to the morning.

1. When does this poem take place?

_____

2. Why are the branches said to be breathing gently?
The branches are breathing gently because they may be asleep or just waking up.

3. Why is the crow's call said to be a "salute to the morning"? Explain this line.

_____

_____

_____

4. What might be the author's meaning in this poem?

_____

_____

_____

Unit 4: Writing Forms
Core Skills Writing 6, SV 9781419039041

Writing a Literary Response, page 2

To write a good literary response, you should:

- support your answers by giving specific examples from the selection.
- support your answers by giving examples from your own experiences.
- connect main ideas or events throughout the selection.
- compare and contrast ideas in the selection with your own experiences.

 Read the story below. Then answer the questions on another sheet of paper. Write complete sentences.

A Friend in Need

I had never really met Old Man Akers. I had heard lots of stories about him. People said he had been badly injured in World War II. Other people said he must have been in prison. Some of my friends said he yelled at them when they threw stuff at him. They said he was from another planet. I just knew him as an old man who hobbled around his yard next door to our house. My mother said, "Jacob, just leave that old man alone."

One day, though, I heard a weak cry for help coming from Mr. Akers's yard. No one else was at home, so I didn't know what to do. I peeked around a tree and saw the old man on the ground, struggling to get up. I immediately hopped over the fence and ran toward him. I didn't even think about what might happen to me. He looked up at me with cloudy eyes and weakly took my hand. I helped him into his house, which was dusty and smelled like old books. He told me a phone number to call, and soon his son arrived to take care of him. I left Old Man Akers's house that day with a different idea about him and about me.

1. Who is the main character of the story?

2. Is the narrator like his friends? Would he throw stuff at Old Man Akers? Explain.

3. Why does the narrator go to help the old man?

4. In the last sentence, the narrator says he gained a different idea about himself that day. What does he mean?

5. If Old Man Akers and the narrator are not really friends, what does the title mean? Explain.

6. Would you go to help Old Man Akers? Tell why or why not.

Writing for Tests

Do you like to take tests? Some people might, but most people don't. A test puts you under pressure. You usually don't have any control over what you must do. And then you're supposed to do your best! Many people especially don't like essay questions. Do you? I didn't think so. But writing on a test can be made easier if you follow these tips.

Prewriting (4 or 5 minutes)

- Is there a time limit? Is there a word limit? Are you allowed to use your textbook? Be sure you understand the directions and just what you are supposed to do.
- Read the essay question carefully. Do you understand it and your goal? Read the question again. If possible, read it aloud.

How did Native Americans adapt to their environment? Give two examples.

- Do not start writing immediately. Remember the prewriting step. You need to plan your writing. If you have 15 minutes to answer the question, spend 4 or 5 minutes prewriting. Then plan to spend 5 or 6 minutes to write and use the remaining time to revise, proofread, and edit.
- What are you asked to do in the question? What writing purpose and pattern should you use to do as asked? Organize the topic in your head. If possible, write an outline of your answer.
- Put some ideas on paper. Freewrite your ideas and facts. Organize your information by numbering the facts in a logical order.

Organizing notes

Inuit—built igloos, traveled to find food   2

Iroquois—built homes of wood and bark, hunted game   1

What is the worst part of a test? What is the best part of a test? Are tests necessary? Why or why not? Write your ideas.

_____

_____

_____

_____

_____

Writing for Tests, page 2

Drafting (5 or 6 minutes)

- Now you are ready to write your first draft. You need a topic sentence. What focus do

  the details provide? _____

- Write the main ideas of the answer in the topic sentence.

Topic sentence

Native Americans had to adapt their housing and eating habits to
their environment.

- Does the topic sentence capture your meaning? Is it a general statement of your ideas?
  If so, continue writing your answer. If not, revise your topic sentence.
- Remember to indent the first sentence in the paragraph.

Write

   Native Americans had to adapt their housing and eating habits to
their environment. The Iroquois lived in the eastern forests where trees
and game animals were plentiful. They built shelters called longhouses
out of wood and bark. They hunted for food. An example of adaptation
to extreme conditions was the Inuit way of life. In the Arctic, many Inuit
built igloos for winter homes. They, too, traveled and hunted in search
of food.

Revising, Proofreading, and Publishing (4 or 5 minutes)

- Read what you have written. Then read the essay question again. Have you answered
  the question completely?
- Are there any facts you should include or delete?
- Is your grammar correct? Have you misspelled any words?
- Is your writing easy to read? Do you have time to rewrite?

**Are there any other strategies you can use to make writing essay questions easier?
Write your ideas. Use another sheet of paper if necessary.**

_____

_____

_____

Name _____ Date _____

Writing to Prompts

Many schools use tests to evaluate students' ability to write. One kind of test uses a writing **prompt,** which requires a written response to a statement, a question, or a picture.

- Read the prompt carefully to help you choose the purpose for writing, the audience, and the form and pattern for writing the essay.
- You may have to write using a time limit or a word limit, so remember to prewrite and plan.
- You may be supplied with paper to plan and write the response.

Complete the writing process for the prompt below. Use another sheet of paper if necessary.

Prompt   You have probably read a history book, and you know what a personal narrative is. Do you think personal narratives are a good way to record history? Tell why or why not.

Organizing notes

_____

_____

_____

Topic sentence

_____

_____

Write

_____

_____

_____

_____

_____

_____

_____

Unit 4: Writing Forms
Core Skills Writing 6, SV 9781419039041

Writing an Informative Report

Are you ready for a challenge? Do you think you can write a report? Keep in mind that your report must be five paragraphs long. You need an introduction paragraph, three body paragraphs that give details, and a conclusion paragraph. Can you write that much? Well, give it a try.

First, you need to choose a topic and a focus. Suppose you are assigned to write a short report on animals. What would you do? You can begin the process by asking yourself some questions. Remember, this is the brainstorming or prewriting part.

What am I supposed to write about? _____

Can I write all about animals in 500 words? No, the topic is too broad. I need a focus. I need to narrow my topic.

What do I know about animals? _____

_____

OK, now you have done a little brainstorming. Most work on an informative report is done before the writing begins. There are many things about animals you could write about. Let's try narrowing some topics.

animals ⟶ mammals ⟶ common features of mammals

animals ⟶ animals by continent ⟶ animals in Australia

animals ⟶ _____ ⟶ _____

Let's say you are going to write a short report on animals in Australia. The first thing you need is a **thesis statement.** It tells what you will write about in the report. The thesis statement usually goes at the end of the introduction.

Thesis statement: Some of the animals in Australia have characteristics that no other animals on Earth have.

Another possible thesis statement: _____

_____

Name _____ Date _____

Taking Notes

Let's say you are reading a **source** about your topic. A source is a place you get information. It may be a book, an encyclopedia, a magazine, a television show, or the Internet. There are many sources to consider for your report.

You find some information you want to use in your report. You decide to take notes. Two ways to take notes are **paraphrases** and **direct quotes.** You can also summarize the information you read.

- You use a **paraphrase** to restate someone else's ideas in your own words. A good paraphrase shows you are thinking about your topic. You are reading carefully.
- To paraphrase, you must first read the source carefully. Then close the source. Think about what you have read. Write your ideas using your own words.
- Copying words from a source and changing a few of them is bad paraphrasing. You must write the information in your own words. You must use your own voice and writing, not someone else's.

Carefully read the information in the sentence below. Next, put a sheet of paper over the sentence. Count to 50. Then, write the sentence in your own words—two different ways! Use another sheet of paper if necessary.

The emu is the largest bird in Australia, standing over 5 feet tall and weighing over 100 pounds.

_____

_____

_____

_____

_____

_____

_____

_____

Core Skills Writing 6, SV 9781419039041

Name _____   Date _____

Direct Quotes

Sometimes the information you find is very important. You can't write the information better in your own words. In this case, you can write a **direct quote.**

- A direct quote uses a group of words as they appear in the source. You copy the words exactly from the source. You put **quotation marks** at each end of the direct quote.
- If the direct quote includes the end of a sentence, the period goes inside the quotation marks.

> A "prehistoric lake left clay and salt" as the water evaporated.
> Death Valley is among the "hottest and driest places in North America."

Do not use many direct quotes in your report. If you do, then you are not doing much writing. You are just copying what someone else has written.

Read the paragraph carefully. Answer each question by writing a direct quote from the paragraph. Remember to enclose the direct quote in quotation marks.

    Another unusual animal native to Australia is the emu. It is a large bird very much like an ostrich. In fact, the emu is the largest bird in Australia, standing over 5 feet tall and weighing over 100 pounds. Even though the emu is a bird, it cannot fly. It weighs too much, and its wings are too small. The emu has long legs and can run as fast as 40 miles an hour.

1. To what other bird is the emu similar? _____

_____

2. How big is the emu? _____

_____

3. How is the emu different from most other birds? _____

_____

4. Why can't the emu fly? _____

_____

Name _____ Date _____

A Writing Plan: Outlining

You have been using writing plans for your paragraphs. You need a writing plan for your report, too. A longer writing plan is called an **outline.** It lists the main ideas of a topic.

- Start your outline with a **thesis statement** that tells the focus of the report.
- Write your main headings and subheadings. These parts tell what goes in each body paragraph of your report.
- Main headings start with a Roman numeral. Subheadings start with a capital letter.
- Each Roman numeral should represent a paragraph.

Thesis statement: Some of the animals in Australia have characteristics that no other animals on Earth have.

I. Kangaroo
   A. Hops
   B. Has a pouch to carry young
   C. Young kangaroo is called a joey

II. Koala
   A. Has a pouch to carry young
   B. Eats only eucalyptus leaves

III. Emu
   A. Very large bird
   B. Cannot fly
   C. Runs fast

 Answer the questions.

1. What would be the topics of the three body paragraphs?

_____

2. What would be a detail from the third body paragraph?

_____

Unit 4: Writing Forms
Core Skills Writing 6, SV 9781419039041

A Writing Plan: Outlining, page 2

Follow these steps to write a good outline.

- Write a thesis statement that tells the focus of the report.
- Write each main idea as a main heading. Use a Roman numeral and a period.
- Write each detail as a subheading. Indent and use a capital letter followed by a period.
- Begin the first word in each line with a capital letter.
- Do not write a *I.* without a *II.* or an *A.* without a *B.*
- Plan one paragraph for each main topic in your outline.
- Order is important. If a process is described, write the details in the order the steps occur.
- Write your report in the same order you have organized it in your outline.

 Use the details in the box to complete the outline.

Long ears	Jackrabbit	Feed at night
Strong hind legs	Kick and bite	
Cottontail	Sharp teeth	

Thesis statement: Rabbits are a common animal with similar features.

    I. Appearance of rabbits

       A. _____

       B. _____

       C. _____

   II. Habits of rabbits

       A. _____

       B. _____

  III. Kinds of rabbits

       A. _____

       B. _____

Name _____ Date _____

Beginning and Ending a Report

An **introduction paragraph** introduces your report. It gives your reader some general information about your topic.

- Write a catchy beginning sentence. Try to grab your reader's interest.
- Name your topic in your introduction.
- Tell some general details about your topic.
- Write a **thesis statement** for your report. A thesis statement is like a topic sentence. It gives the focus of your report. It tells how you have narrowed your topic.

Australia is the only country that is also a continent. Australia also has several unique animals. Many people travel to this island continent just to see the animals. **Some of the animals in Australia have characteristics that no other animals on Earth have.**

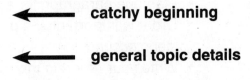

← catchy beginning

← general topic details

← thesis statement

A **conclusion paragraph** ends your report. You don't want to just stop writing after your last body paragraph. You want to let your reader know what he or she has just read in your report.

- Restate your thesis statement in different words.
- Summarize details from your report.
- Tell the reader why the topic is important.

Read the sample introduction paragraph in the box above. Use the introduction paragraph and the outline on page 110 to write a conclusion paragraph. Remember to restate the thesis statement in your own words. Summarize the details about Australian animals. Use another sheet of paper if necessary.

_____

_____

_____

_____

_____

_____

_____

Name _____ Date _____

Writing Your Report

Writing a good informative report takes a lot of time and hard work. You will do better if you have a plan. Follow the steps below to make writing your report easier.

Step 1: Choose a topic. Think about your audience and your purpose.

Step 2: Narrow your topic. Find your focus. Choose a writing pattern. Write a thesis statement.

Step 3: Find some sources. Begin by looking up your topic in an encyclopedia. You can also search on the Internet. Record the names of your sources.

Step 4: Take notes. Remember, you can summarize or paraphrase information. You can also write direct quotes. Be sure your notes are accurate.

Step 5: Build a writing plan. An outline is a good writing plan. Each Roman numeral should be a paragraph in your report.

Step 6: Write an introduction paragraph. Your introduction should have a catchy beginning. It should name your topic and include general details. It should also contain your thesis statement.

Step 7: Write a rough draft of your body paragraphs. Remember to use your writing plan.

Step 8: Write a conclusion paragraph. Remember to restate your thesis in different words. You should also summarize details from your report.

Step 9: Put your report aside for a day or two, if you have time. Then read it again. Read it aloud. What kind of revisions can you make? How can your report be improved? Do you need to add more details? Write another draft.

Step 10: Proofread and edit your second draft. Make corrections.

Step 11: Write your final draft. Be sure to proofread your final draft, too.

Step 12: Publish your report. Include a cover sheet with a title and drawings if possible.

Use the 12 steps above to write an informative report. Start below, and then continue on another sheet of paper.

My topic: _____

Thesis statement: _____

_____

Unit 4: Writing Forms
Core Skills Writing 6, SV 9781419039041

Prewriting Survey

My Purpose

1. What am I writing about?

_____

2. What do I want to say?

_____

_____

3. What is my purpose for writing? Explain.

_____

_____

My Audience

4. Who will be reading my writing? What do I know about my audience?

_____

_____

5. What does my audience already know about my topic? What new information will I tell my audience?

_____

_____

6. How will I share my writing with my audience?

_____

_____

Prewriting Survey, page 2

Writing Purpose and Details

7. Why am I writing? Choose one purpose below and write the details you want to share.

To inform (to give facts about a topic)	Who What Where	When Why How
To express (to share a personal feeling or idea)	What I see What I hear What I touch What I smell What I taste	
To entertain (to make the reader experience an emotion)	Feelings Memories Vivid words Figurative language Stories Poems	
To persuade (to make the reader think or act a certain way)	My claim Details that support my claim	

Writing Pattern

8. Which writing pattern will I use to achieve my purpose?

Main idea and details	Sequence of events	Compare and contrast
Problem and solution	Cause and effect	Summary

Planning

9. Which graphic organizer can help me plan the details of my writing? Circle all that might be useful.

Main idea and details web	Sequence chart	Problem and solution chart
Summary chart	Venn diagram	Cause and effect chart

Name _____ Date _____

Writing Traits Checklist

Title _____

Trait	Strong	Average	Needs Improvement
Ideas			
The main idea of my writing is interesting.			
The topic is just the right size. I have good focus.			
The main idea is written clearly in one sentence.			
I have strong supporting details about the main idea.			
Organization			
The form of writing makes the information clear.			
My writing has a beginning, a middle, and an end.			
The details are in the right order.			
I use transition words to connect my ideas.			
My first sentence catches the reader's interest.			
My last sentence restates the main idea.			
Voice			
I show what I think or feel about the topic.			
I use the right tone for my writing: funny, serious, sad.			
I use words that my audience will understand.			
Word Choice			
I use the five senses to describe things.			
I use strong action words to tell what is happening.			
I use exact words in my writing.			
I use new words in my writing when needed.			

Blackline Masters
Core Skills Writing 6, SV 9781419039041

Name _____ Date _____

Writing Traits Checklist, page 2

Trait	Strong	Average	Needs Improvement
Sentence Fluency			
I have sentences that are short, medium, and long.			
I avoid repeating the same sentence pattern again and again.			
I use the same verb tense throughout the writing.			
I write sentences that begin with different parts of speech.			
Conventions			
All sentences begin with a capital letter.			
All my sentences end with the correct punctuation.			
All subjects and verbs agree with each other.			
All pronouns and nouns agree with each other.			
I use an apostrophe to show possession.			
I use a comma to join two independent clauses joined with *and, or,* or *but.*			
I use quotation marks to write dialogue or a quote.			
I indent the first line of each paragraph.			
Presentation			
My writing has a title.			
I use pictures, charts, or diagrams to support the ideas in my writing.			
The final copy is clean and neat.			
My drawing or writing is neat and easy to read.			
I have a cover and title page.			

Name _____ Date _____

Proofreading Checklist

You should proofread your work before you publish it. When you proofread, you look at your writing for mistakes. Proofread your work several times to search for mistakes. This list will help you proofread.

Capitalization

- [ ] Do all my sentences begin with a capital letter?
- [ ] Are titles and people's names capitalized?
- [ ] Are proper names of places capitalized?
- [ ] Are the months and days of the week capitalized?

Punctuation

- [ ] Does each sentence have the correct end punctuation?
- [ ] Did I use a period at the end of each abbreviation?
- [ ] Did I use a comma to separate items in a series?
- [ ] Did I use a comma correctly to separate a quotation from the rest of the sentence?
- [ ] Did I use quotation marks around dialogue?
- [ ] Did I use quotation marks around a direct quote?
- [ ] Did I use apostrophes to show possession?

Spelling

- [ ] Did I spell all the words correctly?
- [ ] Did I use a dictionary to check words that might be misspelled?
- [ ] Did I use a dictionary to check troublesome words?

Grammar and Usage

- [ ] Do my subjects and verbs agree in number?
- [ ] Do my nouns and pronouns agree in number?
- [ ] Do I have any sentence fragments?
- [ ] Do I have any run-on sentences?
- [ ] Do I have any double negatives?

Blackline Masters
Core Skills Writing 6, SV 9781419039041

Proofreading Marks

Use the marks below to edit your writing.

☰	Use a capital letter.
⊙	Add a period.
∧	Add something.
⋏	Add a comma.
ˇ ˇ	Add quotation marks.
⟋	Cut something.
⋏	Replace something.
⤳	Transpose.
◯	Spell correctly.
¶	Indent paragraph.
╱	Make a lowercase letter.

Name _____ Date _____

Self-Evaluation Checklist

Title _____

	Yes	No

1. Did I take time to prewrite and brainstorm about my topic? _____ _____

2. Did I think about my audience? _____ _____

3. Did I choose the right purpose and form for my topic? _____ _____

4. Do I have good focus about my topic? _____ _____

5. Is my writing clear and easy to understand? _____ _____

6. Is the main idea of each sentence clear and direct? _____ _____

7. Did I present information in a logical order? _____ _____

8. Did I choose interesting and exact words? _____ _____

9. Are my verbs and adjectives lively and interesting? _____ _____

10. Did I add details, examples, facts, explanations, or direct quotes
to strengthen my writing? _____ _____

11. Did I remove unnecessary information? _____ _____

12. Did I follow basic rules for capitalization, punctuation, spelling,
grammar, and usage? _____ _____

13. Did I link events and ideas with transition words? _____ _____

14. Do my sentences have good rhythm and flow? _____ _____

15. Did I revise confusing parts to make them clearer? _____ _____

16. Did I choose a title that grabs my reader's attention? _____ _____

17. Is my writing neat and easy to read? _____ _____

18. Have I done my best work on this piece of writing? _____ _____

Blackline Masters
Core Skills Writing 6, SV 9781419039041

Main Idea and Details Web

Write the main idea in the oval. Write five strong details in the circles. Think about specific and lively words that you could use in your writing to tell about the details. Write these words in the rectangles.

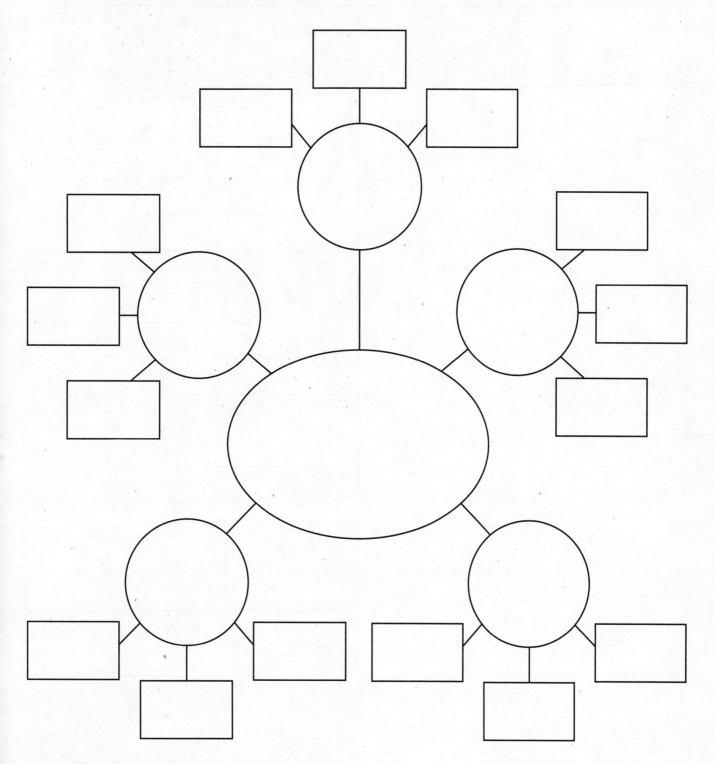

Summary Chart

➤ **Write the details on the left side of the chart. Write a summary on the right side of the chart. Try to include all the information in as few sentences as you can.**

Who	Summary
	_____
	_____
What	_____
	_____
	_____
Where	_____
	_____
	_____
When	_____
	_____
	_____
Why	_____
	_____
	_____
How	_____
	_____

Problem and Solution Chart

➤ **Name the problem in the first box. Then write details about the problem. Name the solution that would fix the problem. Give details to explain why the solution would work.**

Problem	Details about Problem *(Why is it a problem?)*

Solution	Details about Solution *(Why is it a good solution?)*

Cause and Effect Chart

➤ **Write what happened in the Effect box. Write the reason it happened in the Cause box.**

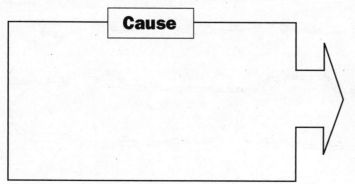

Cause   **Effect**

Paragraph Structure Chart

Use the graphic organizer to plan your paragraph. Write your topic sentence and concluding sentence on the pieces of bread. Write your details between the slices.

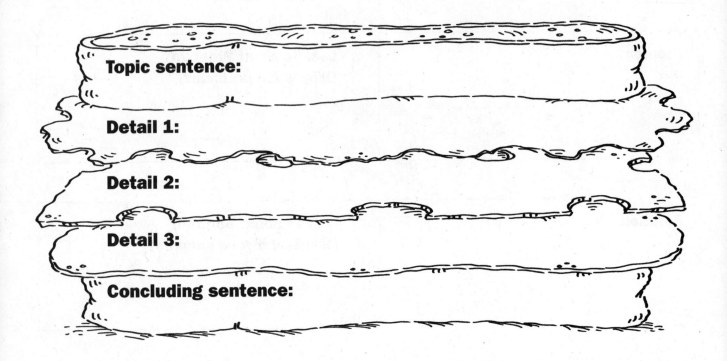

Topic sentence:

Detail 1:

Detail 2:

Detail 3:

Concluding sentence:

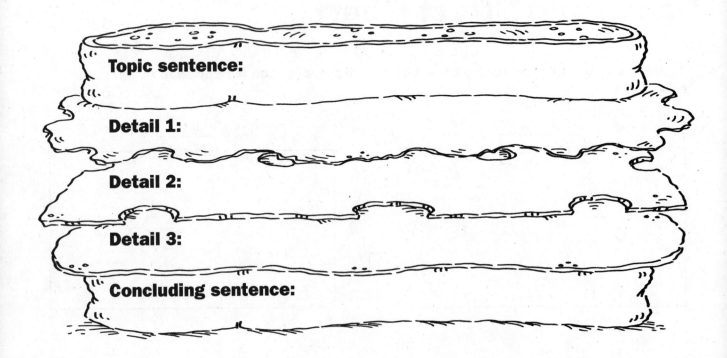

Topic sentence:

Detail 1:

Detail 2:

Detail 3:

Concluding sentence:

Glossary

action verb (page 14) a verb that shows action

active verb (page 55) a verb that shows action done by the subject of the sentence

adjective (page 15) a word that modifies a noun or pronoun

adjective phrase (page 40) a prepositional phrase that serves as an adjective

adverb (page 15) a word that modifies a verb, an adjective, or another adverb

adverb phrase (page 40) a prepositional phrase that serves as an adverb

audience (page 10) the ones who will read what you write

brainstorming (page 17) to think about ideas for your writing

cause (page 80) why something has happened

characters (page 90) real or made-up people or animals in a narrative

claim (page 99) a statement about which side of the issue you support

clause (page 37) a group of related words that includes a subject and a predicate

coherence (page 69) when the parts of a paragraph have a logical order

comma (page 50) a mark of punctuation used to separate the parts of a compound sentence or a series

comma splice (page 66) a sentence error caused when two complete sentences are joined with only a comma

common noun (page 13) a word that names any person, place, or thing; begins with a small letter

compare (page 79) to show how two things are alike

complete predicate (page 24) the simple predicate and all the words that describe it

complete subject (page 24) the simple subject and all the words that describe it

complex sentence (page 50) a sentence that contains one independent clause and one or more dependent clauses

compound predicate (page 42) a predicate containing two or more simple predicates

compound sentence (page 50) a sentence that is made up of two or more simple sentences

compound subject (page 42) a subject containing two or more simple subjects

concluding sentence (page 69) restates the main idea and summarizes the information in the paragraph

conclusion paragraph (page 112) the last paragraph in a report or long piece of writing

conjunction (page 16) a word that connects words or groups of words

connective (page 16) a word that joins parts of a sentence

contrast (page 79) to show how two things are different

conventions (page 21) the rules of grammar and writing

coordinate conjunction (page 41) a conjunction that joins two words, two phrases, or two clauses of equal rank

declarative sentence (page 47) a sentence that makes a statement

dependent clause (page 44) a clause that is not a complete sentence; it must be attached to an independent clause

definition (page 95) the meaning of a word

describe (page 87) to tell what something is like; to paint a picture with words

details (page 32) words that tell whose, which, when, where, and how about the main idea

detail sentences (page 69) body sentences that tell more about the main idea of a paragraph

dialogue (page 92) words said by characters in a narrative

direct object (page 27) receiver of the action in a sentence

direct quote (page 109) copying words exactly from a source

draft (page 23) a version of a piece of writing

drafting (page 17) writing a version of your ideas on a topic

edit (page 23) to correct errors you have made in writing

effect (page 80) something that has been caused to happen

emphasis (page 69) when the important ideas in a paragraph are stressed

entertain (page 11) to please or amuse the reader

exclamation mark (page 48) a mark of punctuation used at the end of an exclamatory sentence

exclamatory sentence (page 48) a sentence that shows excitement or strong feeling

express (page 11) to tell your personal feelings

fact (page 96) a statement that can be proved

figurative language (page 60) words used to compare unlike things

focus (page 71) to narrow a topic

fused sentence (page 65) a sentence error caused when two complete sentences are joined with no mark of punctuation

future tense verb (page 56) a verb that tells what will happen in the future

helping verb (page 28) a verb that comes before the main verb in a sentence

ideas (page 19) what you have to say or write about a topic

imperative sentence (page 48) a sentence that makes a request or gives a command

indent (page 70) move in five spaces from the left margin

independent clause (page 37) a clause that is a complete sentence and shows a complete thought

inform (page 11) to tell facts about a topic

information paragraph (page 96) tells facts about one topic

interrogative sentence (page 47) a sentence that asks a question

introduction paragraph (page 112) the first paragraph in a report or long piece of writing

inverted order (page 62) changing the order of the subject and the verb in a sentence

issue (page 99) an idea that people disagree about

journal (page 12) a record of daily events

linking verb (page 29) a verb that links the subject to a noun or an adjective in the complete predicate

literary response (page 102) writing your ideas about a literary reading selection

main idea (page 25) what a piece of writing is mainly about

metaphor (page 60) figurative language that compares two things by speaking of one thing as if it were another; does not use *like* or *as*

modifier (page 15) a word or group of words that changes the meaning of another word

narrate (page 90) tell about a sequence of events

narrative (page 90) a factual or fictional story

noun (page 13) a word that names a person, place, or thing

object of the preposition (page 39) the noun or pronoun that follows a preposition

object pronoun (page 13) used as the object of a sentence

opinion (page 96) someone's belief that cannot be proved

organization (page 19) the way you arrange the ideas you are writing

outcome (page 90) the ending of a narrative

outline (page 110) a writing plan for the content of a report

paragraph (page 69) a group of sentences that tells about one main idea

paraphrase (page 108) to restate someone else's ideas in your own words

passive verb (page 55) a verb that shows being and not action

past tense verb (page 56) a verb that tells what happened in the past

period (page 47) a mark of punctuation used at the end of a declarative sentence

personal narrative (page 91) a story about something you have done

personification (page 61) giving human qualities to nonhuman things

persuade (page 11) to try to convince the reader to do something

persuasive paragraph (page 99) tries to make the reader do something

phrase (page 37) a group of words that does not have a subject or a predicate

plural verb (page 26) a verb that agrees with a plural subject

predicate (page 24) the part of a sentence that tells what the subject is or does

predicate adjective (page 29) an adjective linked to a subject by a linking verb

predicate nominative (page 29) a noun or pronoun linked to a subject by a linking verb

preposition (page 16) a word that shows the relation of a noun or pronoun to another word in a sentence

prepositional phrase (page 39) a phrase made up of a preposition, its object, and any other words

present tense verb (page 56) a verb that tells what is happening now

presentation (page 21) the way words and pictures look on the page

prewriting (page 17) to think about what and why you are writing

problem (page 81) something that is wrong

prompt (page 106) a question or situation given as a writing assignment

pronoun (page 13) a word that takes the place of a noun

proofreading (page 18) searching for errors you have made in writing

proper noun (page 13) a word that names a particular person, place, or thing; begins with a capital letter

publishing (page 18) sharing your writing with others

purpose (page 11) your reason for writing

question mark (page 47) a mark of punctuation used at the end of an interrogative sentence

quotation marks (page 92) punctuation marks that are placed at each end of dialogue or a direct quote

revising (page 18) to think more about what you have written to make it better

run-on sentence (page 65) a sentence error caused by incorrect punctuation

sentence (page 24) a group of words that tells a complete thought

sentence fluency (page 21) the rhythm and flow of your sentences

sentence fragment (page 64) a part of a sentence that does not tell a complete idea

sequence (page 78) a series of events in order

series (page 51) a list of three or more words or items

setting (page 90) where and when the events of a narrative take place

simile (page 60) figurative language that compares two things by using *like* or *as*

simple predicate (page 25) the main verb in the complete predicate

simple sentence (page 50) a complete sentence that contains only one complete thought

simple subject (page 25) the main noun or pronoun in the complete subject

singular verb (page 26) a verb that agrees with a singular subject

solution (page 81) the way to fix a problem

source (page 108) a place to find information

subject (page 24) who or what a sentence is about

subject pronoun (page 13) used as the subject of a sentence

subordinate conjunction (page 44) a conjunction that joins a dependent clause to an independent clause

summarize (page 77) to tell the key details of an event or a piece of writing

summary (page 77) the key details of a piece of writing

tense (page 56) the time a verb tells

thesis statement (page 107) a sentence that tells the focus of a report or long piece of writing

time-order words (page 78) transition words that show movement in time

topic (page 17) what you are writing about

topic sentence (page 69) tells the main idea of the paragraph

understood subject (page 48) the subject (*you*) of an imperative sentence that does not appear in the sentence; however, the subject is understood to be *you*

unity (page 69) when all the parts of a paragraph tell about one main idea

unnecessary information (page 82) information that does not belong in a paragraph

verb (page 14) a word that shows action or connects the subject to another word in a sentence

verb phrase (page 28) the main verb and its helpers in a sentence

verb tense (page 56) the time a verb tells

voice (page 20) the way a writer "speaks" to the reader through writing

word choice (page 20) the words you pick to express your ideas

writing traits (page 19) skills, features, or characteristics of writing

Core Skills Writing
Grade 6, Answer Key

Student answers will vary on the pages not included in this Answer Key. Accept all reasonable answers.

Page 9
1. D
2. B
3. B
4. A

Page 10
Answers will vary. Possible answers include:
1. the writer, close friends
2. adults, citizens, people at a city meeting
3. friends, family members
4. friends, family, a book club, newspaper readers
5. friends, family members
6. adults, citizens, people at a city meeting

Page 11
Answers may vary.
1. B
2. A
3. C
4. D

Page 16
Answers may vary.
1. after
2. and
3. but
4. because
5. before
6. or
7.–8. Answers will vary.

Page 18
A furry bear fished in the mountain stream. Correct order: 5, 2, 4, 3 ,1

Page 24
1. no
2. yes
3. no
4. yes
5. no
6.–10. Answers will vary.

Page 37
1. Clause: Everyone should know; Phrase: about medical emergencies

2. Clause: You can injure yourself; Phrase: in an accident
3. Clause: Someone may be cut; Phrase: by a knife
4. Clause: A person could break a bone; Phrase: in a fall
5. Clause: people sometimes choke; Phrase: In restaurants
6. Clause: You can help people; Phrase: with first aid
7. Clause: The phone number . . . is 911; Phrase: for emergencies
8. Clause: Maybe you will be a doctor; Phrase: in the future

Page 43
Answers will vary. Check that the verb is correct.
1. live
2. makes
3. are
4.–6. Answers will vary.

Page 45
Answers may vary.
1. More important information: Cleopatra ruled Egypt with her brother.
Sentence: Cleopatra ruled Egypt with her brother until he seized the throne.
2. More important information: Cleopatra regained her throne.
Sentence: Cleopatra regained her throne because Julius Caesar helped her.
3. More important information: Mark Antony ruled Rome.
Sentence: Mark Antony ruled Rome after Julius Caesar died.
4. More important information: Antony went to Egypt.
Sentence: Antony went to Egypt, where he lived for several years.

Page 49
1. ?
2. ! or .
3. . or !
4. . or !
5.–10. Answers will vary. Check that sentences fulfill the directions.

Page 53
Answers may vary. Possible answer:

Carley and Marley looked down at the hole in the ground. They couldn't see much. Marley scratched his head and wondered what to do. Meanwhile, Carley ran to the house and returned with a flashlight. Marley and Carley nodded at each other. Carley shined the light down the hole. Suddenly a red rabbit jumped from the hole and started to yell at them.

Page 56
Answers may vary. Check that verbs are the correct tense.
1. works
2. built
3. will start
4. likes
5. watches
6. saw
7. fell
8. will rain
9. will play
10. hit

Page 64
Sentences 3 and 4 are not fragments.

Page 65
Answers may vary.
1. Aristotle lived in ancient Greece. He became a great philosopher.
2. Plato was a famous philosopher, and Aristotle attended his school.
3. Aristotle became famous himself, and many people studied his work.
4. Aristotle taught Alexander the Great before Alexander became king of Macedonia.
5. Aristotle started his own school when he received money from Alexander.

Page 66
Answers may vary.
1. Friction makes meteors incredibly hot, so they burn up miles above Earth's surface.
2. Some large meteors do not burn up completely. They are called meteorites.

3. A meteorite exploded over Siberia, where it created more than 200 craters.
4. A meteorite crashed there perhaps 50,000 years ago, or it may have fallen earlier.

Page 68
Answers may vary.
1. Look at those two bears in that airplane.
2. They're flying just above the treetops in a blue biplane.
3. Those two bears have to be crazy!
4. Now they're flying above the cotton clouds.

Page 69
Students should suggest that the first paragraph is better. The second paragraph does not stay on topic.

Page 70
Answers may vary.
1. word origins
2. From her name come many words we use every day.
3. Answers will vary but should not be the second or last sentence in the paragraph.
4. As you can see, words can have very interesting origins.

Page 82
Reasons will vary but should suggest the unnecessary information is not about the topic.
1. Unnecessary information: Cattle are not very smart animals, and they often moo too loud. The cowhands ride horses, too.
2. Unnecessary information: Shallow water is good for swimming, though.

Page 84
Errors include indenting, spelling, capitalization, and punctuation. The correct paragraph follows:

Can you imagine an animal that seems to be part mammal, part reptile, and part bird? If you succeed, you will probably imagine an animal like the platypus. In appearance, the platypus most closely resembles a duck. Like a duck, it has a bill. It also has webbed feet, fur, and a flat tail like a beaver's. Most mammals are warm-blooded.

Their temperature remains the same regardless of the temperature of their surroundings. A platypus is cold-blooded. Like a reptile, its body temperature changes with the temperature of its surroundings.

Page 93
Answers may vary.
1. Shelley's new house was similar to her old house in some ways, but it was different, too.
2. Both houses had three bedrooms and two bathrooms, a fireplace in the living room, and a separate dining room.
3. The old house was about 100 years old, but the new house had just been built. The old house had two stories, but the new house had only one level. The old house had hardwood floors, but the new house had carpeting.

Page 96
Reasons will vary.
1. opinion; do not include
2. fact; include
3. fact; include
4. opinion; do not include
5. opinion; do not include

Page 102
Answers may vary.
1. The poem takes place at sunrise.
3. The crow's call seems to welcome the coming day.
4. The author's meaning may be that sunrise is a special time of day.

Page 103
Answers may vary.
1. The main character is the narrator, a boy named Jacob.
2. The boy is not really like his friends because he probably would not throw things at the old man. He seems to feel sorry for the old man and is willing to help him instead of being mean to him.
3. The narrator seems to be a caring and considerate young man.
4. The narrator may feel he has overcome his fears and can be a kind and responsible young adult.
5. In a sense, any person in need can be a friend. As the old saying goes, "a friend in need is a friend indeed."
6. Answers will vary.

Page 109
Answers may vary.
1. "It is a large bird very much like an ostrich."
2. "In fact, the emu is the largest bird in Australia, standing over 5 feet tall and weighing over 100 pounds."
3. "Even though the emu is a bird, it cannot fly."
4. "It weighs too much, and its wings are too small."

Page 110
Answers may vary.
1. kangaroos, koalas, and emus
2. Answers will vary but should include one of the details about emus.

Page 111
Outlines may vary.
 I. Appearance of rabbits
    A. Long ears
    B. Sharp teeth
    C. Strong hind legs
 II. Habits of rabbits
    A. Kick and bite
    B. Feed at night
III. Kinds of rabbits
    A. Cottontail
    B. Jackrabbit

Answer Key
Core Skills Writing 6, SV 9781419039041